Big Game on a Budget

TRACY BREEN

Big Game on a Budget

Copyright © 2015 by Tracy Breen

published by Tracy Breen Outdoors LLC

All rights reserved. No part of this book may be reproduced or transmitted in any form by any means, electronic or mechanical or otherwise, without the prior written permission of the publisher.

All images are copyright by Tracy Breen, except those used with permission of the copyright holder.

All persons, product names, trademarks, and copyright materials identified or presented in this book are used in an editorial fashion only and with no intention of infringement of the trademark or copyright. No such use, or the use of any trade name, is intended to convey endorsement or other affiliation with this book.

Cover design, book production, and editorial services by Reaser Brand Communications, LLC

ISBN: 1506141900
ISBN-13: 978-1506141909

visit **tracybreen.com**

DEDICATION

First, I would like to thank my Lord and Savior, Jesus Christ. Without him, none of what I have accomplished would have been possible. He truly has taken my lemons and made lemonade.

Next, I would like to thank my lovely bride, Angie—a.k.a. Angeline. She has always been there to encourage my crazy dreams. When I was 19, I told her I wanted to make a living as a writer. Many laughed at that dream. She, on the other hand, helped me succeed and today, almost two decades later, she is still by my side, encouraging me.

Proverbs 31:

10 *A wife of noble character who can find?*
She is worth far more than rubies.

11 *Her husband has full confidence in her*
and lacks nothing of value.

12 *She brings him good, not harm,*
all the days of her life.

CONTENTS

	INTRODUCTION 7
1	BLACK BEARS 11
2	TRAVELING FOR BIG BUCKS 21
3	MOOSE HUNTING 29
4	ELK ON A SHOESTRING 37
5	FULLY GUIDED VS. DROP-CAMP HUNTING ... 43
6	PERSISTANCE PAYS 51
7	CARIBOU HUNTING 57
8	HOG HUNTING IN TEXAS 63
9	THE TRAVELING TURKEY HUNTER 69
10	PHYSICAL CONDITIONING 101 77
11	DRAWING TAGS 81
	EPILOGUE 89
	APPENDIX 91

INTRODUCTION

I can still remember reading every hunting magazine my dad subscribed to when I was a kid. Magazines including *Bowhunter*, *Bowhunting World*, *Petersen's Bowhunting*, and *Outdoor Life* were my window into the outdoor world. I dreamed about one day going on hunting trips like the writers in those magazines. I dreamed of going to places like Alaska to hunt moose and caribou. I dreamed about chasing whitetails in places like Illinois and Kansas. I longed to hunt and fish in Canada. As a kid, such trips seemed like a pipe dream. In my early adulthood, they seemed even more like a dream. Money and time were two things I did not have in abundance. Between paying the bills and a little vacation time, going on hunting trips seemed like something that would never happen.

In my twenties, I became associated with God's Great Outdoors, an outdoor radio ministry. Through this ministry, I connected to the outdoor industry and eventually started writing for outdoor publications. At the age of 23, I thought it was time I try to scrape together a few pennies to go on a hunting trip. My very first trip was to Idaho to hunt elk. My wife and I didn't have much money, but we saved so I could go chase elk. In September of 2001, I boarded a plane and headed west.

My first elk hunt was exhilarating, with excitement, screaming bulls, and long walks in the wilderness, but I did not have a shot opportunity. I learned a lot about elk hunting and, more importantly, figured out that although many believe you need to have deep pockets to go on hunting trips, the truth is a person on a peanut butter-and-jelly budget can hunt almost anywhere. All they need is a little bit of money, a little bit of time, and a desire to hunt.

Over the last decade, I have hunted and fished in dozens of states and several Canadian provinces, all on the income of a freelance writer. Yes, I have been on some guided hunts, but many of my favorite hunting trips have been low-budget affairs where the staple of my diet was Ramen noodles and peanut butter sandwiches. My gear was anything but new and fancy. I have created memories on these low-budget hunts that I will never forget. I still remember my first backcountry elk hunt, where my friend and I packed a lightweight tipi, a week's worth of food, our bows, and a few other gadgets, and hunted miles off the road for close to two weeks. On that particular trip, I lost 15 pounds, didn't kill anything but time, but learned a lot about what it takes to hunt the backcountry. I have been on many successful trips since that probably wouldn't have been successful if it weren't for what I learned in the rugged Idaho mountains.

Hunting big game on a budget is all about adventure and creating memories. Trust me, if you choose to hunt on your own or go on drop camp hunts, you will be in for the time of your life versus paying someone to take you. When you hunt on your own, you have to be a detective to figure out where the animals are. You have to be willing to work, willing to hike the extra mile, and willing to go to lengths most hunters are unwilling to go. In return, you will feel more pride, joy, and excitement than you would ever feel on a guided hunt. If you choose to hunt on your own, you are choosing adventure over filled tags, because when hunting on your own, you won't always be as successful as you would be if you hunted with an outfitter.

I am okay with that.

If you are okay with eating a few bowls of tag soup in return for the adventure that comes with an unguided hunt (because when you fill a tag you will know you earned it), continue reading! This book is written for the guy who wants to chase big game animals, create lasting memories with friends and family, and do it all without breaking the bank.

Tracy Breen

1

BLACK BEARS

The most sought-after big game animal in North America is, without question, the whitetail deer. Hunters can't get enough of them. Nearly every bowhunter dreams of putting an arrow through a monster buck. As a result, every year thousands of hunters pay outfitters in hopes of tagging a trophy. The downside of hunting whitetails is that even when you pay an outfitter, the chances of taking a trophy class animal are slim. Many outfitters have around a 30- to 40-percent success rate on whitetail hunts. It isn't the fault of the outfitter. Killing trophy bucks with or without an outfitter is difficult. And if that's not challenging enough, harvesting a trophy-class elk, mule deer, or moose on a guided hunt can be even more difficult.

The black bear, on the other hand, is the hidden gem often overlooked by hunters. Although this book is largely about going on unguided hunts, I will make a few exceptions in this discussion. For one reason, it is relatively inexpensive to hunt black bears even when hunting with an outfitter, plus the success rate for black bear hunts is extremely high. In fact, many outfitters boast almost a 100-percent success rate, which is why a black bear hunt is a great option for hunters on a tight budget.

Let's face the fact: most hunters want to go on guided hunts in distant places for two reasons—they want to tag a trophy and experience the adventure. There's something about hunting in another state or country that is exciting. Maybe it's because many of us grew up reading the adventures of Fred Bear and we hoped we could one day hunt in similar exotic locations. Fortunately, hunters looking for adventure will be happy with black bear hunting. You will have fun and likely come home with a trophy.

If you have not been on a guided hunt away from home and yearn to do so, consider the black bear for your first hunt expedition. Furthermore, guided black bear hunts are often more affordable than whitetail hunts.

PRICED RIGHT, HIGH SUCCESS RATES

My first black bear hunt took place in Quebec, Canada, in 2008. It was a guided hunt, and of the nine or ten of us in camp, only two hunters went home without having taken a bear. That's a success rate of over 80-percent. I went home with a 300+ pound bear that was quite large for the area we were hunting. The hunt cost $900 for an entire week of hunting. Lodging and bait sites were included in that price. We had to provide our own food, but that wasn't a big deal because each cabin had a kitchen.

Jack Coad, a pro staff member for many companies in the outdoor industry, has taken several bears in Quebec.

"I enjoy hunting black bears," Coad explained, "and I get a bear

BIG GAME ON A BUDGET

almost every year. I get to experience the Canadian wilderness, which is awesome."

Coad and many of his friends have been hunting with this particular outfitter for over a decade. Their walls are covered in bear rugs and bear mounts, proving that you don't have to spend a lot of money to experience some phenomenal hunting.

A BEAR HUNT FOR EVERY BUDGET

There are bear hunts available for almost any sportsman's budget. You can find several guided bear hunts that cost about $1,000, as well as those that cost thousands. It just depends on what you are looking for in a bear hunt. If you are looking for a big bear, one of the best options is to hunt in the Canadian province of Saskatchewan. You might pay $2,500 or more for your hunt, but you may come home with a large, 400-pound-plus bruin with a head the size of a watermelon.

A friend of mine owns an outfitter business in Saskatchewan called Delta Big Game Outfitters. His guided bear hunts last five days and cost $3,000. Almost every hunter who enters his camp gets a shot at a bear, and many of those are color-phase bears, which is something many hunters want.

Now how many whitetail camps do you know where you can spend $3,000 with the almost certain guarantee of a shot opportunity?

BEAR HUNTING OPTIONS
Baiting

There several styles of bear hunting you can choose. The most popular form is to hunt over bait. If this style of hunting interests you, ask your intended outfitter how far in advance they bait before putting hunters on a stand. Your best chance for success is hunting over established bait sites. I've been in camps that started baiting a few days before I arrived, and that's bad news for hunters. You want to hunt a bait station that bears are accustomed to feeding on.

Another question to ask your outfitter is if their bait sites are set up specifically for bowhunters. Are the bait piles a long distance from the treestand or positioned up close and personal? Up close and personal is definitely the preferred set up for archers.

There are many reasons to hunt bears over bait. First, bears have a sweet tooth, and enjoy eating donuts, cookies, and fish. After they discover a bait station, they often visit it daily, which makes tagging one with a bow easier than going out and looking for them. Second, when hunting over bait, your treestand can be set up to allow you to hunt the bait with the wind in your face. Many outfitters know their area's prevailing wind direction and place their stands accordingly. Third, hunting over bait provides the potential to see many bears, and this is good for many reasons. It allows you to get used to seeing bears and judging their size so when you see a large one, you'll know it.

Many Canadian treestands are not very safe. Bring your own, if possible.

The downside of baiting is the fact that you are baiting an animal. Some people don't like baiting any big game animal. If you fall into that category, there are other options for hunting bears.

Dogs

Another popular style of bear hunting that offers a high success rate and doesn't cost much money is hunting bears with hounds. Hunting bears with dogs adds a lot of adventure and excitement to the hunt. Nothing beats chasing after barking dogs when they are hot on the trail of big black bear.

Angie Denny from Table Mountain Outfitters in Idaho knows a good deal about this form of bear hunting.

BIG GAME ON A BUDGET

"Chasing bears with hounds is very exciting," says Denny. "The success rate is close to 100 percent. Last year we had about twenty-three hunters in camp; twenty-one of them went home with bears."

Table Mountain Outfitters has a unique bear hunting operation.

"We hunt bears in the morning with dogs and over baits in the evening. By offering both options, hunters get to experience two different styles of hunting. Our high success rate is partially due to the fact that we hunt with hounds," Denny added.

If you hunt where Table Mountain Outfitters is located, you get to experience hunting out West, which is a dream come true for many eastern hunters. The advantage of bear hunting in the West is you don't have to walk as much as you would if you were hunting elk. The success rate of bears is much higher than the success rate for elk.

Spot-And-Stalk

Another, more adventurous bear hunting option is spot-and-stalk. This style of hunting is popular in Alaska because you can hunt without a guide (unlike in the Canadian provinces), and because Alaska is home to some large bears.

I have several friends who regularly spot-and-stalk bears. They typically glass the terrain for hours looking for bears feeding on berries or salmon. Once they spot one big enough to kill, they stalk it to within lethal shooting distance.

My father-in-law did this while we were caribou hunting in Quebec. He used a gun for that hunt, but the method is the same. We spotted his bear hundreds of yards away from us feeding on wild blueberries. While the bear was occupied with dinner, we slipped in on him and, needless to say, the blueberries were his final meal.

In Alaska, many hunters who want to spot-and-stalk bears on their own get dropped off in the bush by floatplane in an area full of the critters. They camp in tents and hunt during the day. If you are willing to spend a little extra money, you can stay on a houseboat and come to shore each day to hunt black bears that are gorging themselves on salmon. Coastal black bears that eat large amounts of salmon tend to be larger than bears that live inland.

Trapping

One unique way to hunt black bears is to trap them. In Maine, you can hire an outfitter and they will set traps near bait sites. You trap them the old-fashioned way—in foothold traps. This style of trapping and hunting is especially effective on large bears because they often feed on bait in the middle of the night. If you were to trap a large bear, you would then shoot it with your bow.

LOWER-48 STRATEGIES

If you are the do-it-yourself kind of hunter, there are many bear hunting options available, and many states that offer bear hunting. In Michigan, we have a healthy bear population, but you must apply for a tag. Getting a tag in a good unit can take several years. Once you draw, you can bait bears yourself, hire someone to bait them for you, or run hounds. I know several hunters who have taken 500-plus pound bears. Save your pennies and you can easily purchase a hunt for $1,000 or less.

Many states, including Wisconsin and North and South Carolina, offer great bear hunting where you can successfully hunt on your own with a little research and several hundred dollars.

One of my favorite places to hunt regardless of what I am going after is the American West. States such as Colorado and New Mexico have large bear populations. One popular bear hunting method in this region is to sit over a water hole early in the morning or in the evening and wait for the bears to come in for a drink. By placing a scouting camera over a water hole, you can quickly find out if and when bears are visiting.

A friend of mine who lives in Colorado has hunted bears over dead cattle carcasses.

"Many ranchers are not fond of bears, so sometimes if they have had a cow die, they will let you hunt over the carcass," says Matt Guedes. "This is a very effective way to hunt bears."

BIG GAME ON A BUDGET

CALLING

Sometimes you can call black bears into shooting range with predator calls. An outfitter isn't needed for this style of hunting. Buy an electronic caller or use a mouth call that sounds like a fawn or cub in distress.

Lawrence Taylor from Knight & Hale Game Calls has had great success when using predator calls on black bears.

"The key to success when using predator calls on bears is calling nonstop for several minutes at a time," Taylor said. Bears lose interest quickly. If you call a lot, they come and investigate. If you stop calling, they walk away.

Using a predator call is just another option when chasing bears on a budget.

There are no guarantees when hunting, especially when bowhunting, but the black bear could be the most bowhunter-friendly animal on the planet. They are easy to bait, die quickly when hit in the right spot, and they live almost everywhere, including in some of the most wild lands in North America. If you want to go on a hunting adventure that doesn't break the bank yet offers a high chance of success, nothing compares to hunting a black bear. Regardless of whether you choose to hunt over bait, with hounds, spot-and-stalk, or participate in a bear drive like they do in Pennsylvania, one thing is certain—you'll have fun doing it.

MUST-HAVE GEAR

Whether you are hunting with or without an outfitter, there are several things you should bring to bear camp. Below are a few of my must-have items.

Treestand

Bring your own treestand. Many outfitters say they have treestands placed for bowhunters, but that is not always the case. I've sat in treestands made from old plywood and pine branches that looked like they were built when JFK was elected President. Bring a comfortable climber that will allow you to hang your stand where you want. Being comfortable is important when sitting for hours. Canadian outfitters are notorious for building homemade treestands that double as death traps.

Scouting Camera

A scouting camera, hung over a bait site, lets you know when and where to sit. Having a scouting camera on hand is the only reason I stayed an extra day while hunting in Quebec a few years ago. That extra day resulted in me killing the bear on page 11.

A scouting camera is a must-have when bear hunting. It allows you to pattern the bears.

Scent-Reduction

Bring a carbon suit, such as a Scent-Lok or a Scent-Blocker suit, or spray your clothing and gear daily with an odor-eliminating spray. Bears have amazing noses, and the big ones are especially sensitive to human odor (how do you think they got so big?). If you become a scent-free fanatic while bear hunting, your chances of success will likely improve.

Bear Target

Bring a bear target of some type with you. The vitals on a bear

BIG GAME ON A BUDGET

are not the same as the vitals on a deer. If you get used to shooting at a bear target, you'll be better prepared when the big moment arrives. One inexpensive option is to buy a face target for your Block-style target. Master Target and Maple Leaf Press make great targets that show the vitals.

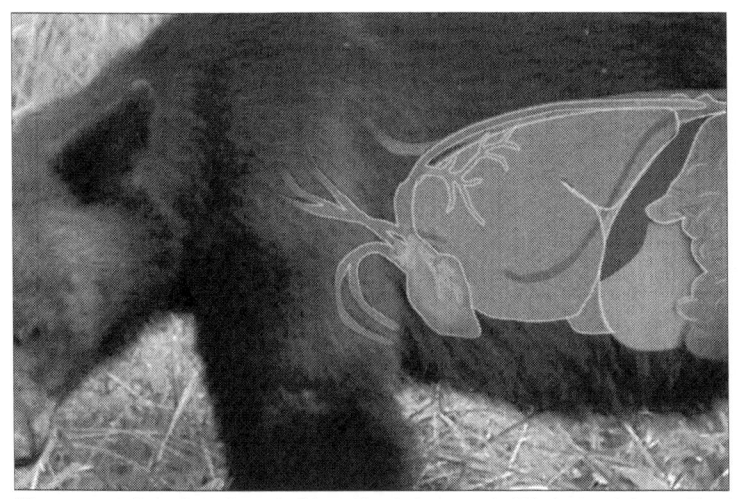

Here you can easily see the vitals on a back bear. Choosing a spot can be difficult when aiming at a big black blob. (photo courtesy MasterTarget, master-target.com)

Bug Gear

Don't leave home without a bug suit and a Thermacell. The bugs can be horrible during spring bear season. If the mosquitoes and black flies are bad, you may have a difficult time staying in the stand all day. Remember, you can't kill a bear in camp!

Tracy Breen

The author with a budget buck.

2

TRAVELING FOR BIG BUCKS

Most deer hunters dream of harvesting a monster buck. Unfortunately, most of these dreams go unfulfilled. There are many reasons hunters don't get their once-in-a-lifetime buck—most prominent among them are a lack of time and money to pursue those dreams. When hunters ogle trophy whitetails on the cover of their favorite magazine or watch them being taken on their favorite hunting show, most don't realize that those bucks are quite often taken with the help of an outfitter. That's not to say, however, that spending oodles of money with an outfitter is the only way to tag a big buck.

GO WHERE THE BIG BUCKS ROAM

Joel Maxfield, Vice President of Marketing for Mathews Archery, has hunted whitetails across the country with outfitters and on his own. Maxfield has proven that hunters don't need tons of money to tag a large buck; they just need to be where the bucks live.

"Hunters who are serious about tagging a mature whitetail don't need much money; they just need to be willing to travel," Maxfield explained. "West of the Mississippi River, the chances of running into a large buck increase dramatically. There isn't as much hunting pressure, and bucks often reach four or five years of age on public and private ground. Getting an opportunity at a mature whitetail is much easier in the Midwest or out West than it is in eastern states that receive lots of hunting pressure."

DO YOUR HOMEWORK

To increase his odds, Maxfield does plenty of homework before going on a hunt.

"I typically buy topo maps or aerial photographs in the states I want to hunt [in order] to narrow down my search," Maxfield said. "Then I head to the hunting area a few days before I plan to hunt and begin scouting. I hunt private and public land, and have been very successful on both."

In the fall of 2009, Maxfield arrowed four mature bucks. Most of them didn't cost more than the price of the tag, fuel, and lodging.

KNOCK ON DOORS

A few of Maxfield's favorite states to hunt in are North Dakota, South Dakota, and Kansas.

"Getting tags in these states is easy, so if I find a great hunting spot, I can return there every year," Maxfield noted.

When scouting, he often knocks on the doors of farmers and asks for permission. "Farmers west of the Mississippi are different from most folks. They don't mind giving hunters permission to hunt. I get turned down occasionally, but most of the time I get permission to hunt. When farmers say no, I go down the road and ask the next guy. One year a farmer who owned thousands of acres said I couldn't hunt. I found out that he doesn't allow anyone to hunt on his property. A farmer down the road gave me permission, so I ended up hunting next to this massive piece of ground that was off limits to hunters. It was like hunting next to a state park.

BEGINNERS LUCK

I've always thought that hunters need lots of time to scout and hunt when traveling to increase the odds of tagging a buck. Maxfield said that's not always the case.

"I shot some of my greatest bucks on the first day of a hunt in a place I had never been before. Much of the farmland I get permission to hunt isn't difficult to scout. There is wide-open ground and little cover. Locating deer in this type of terrain is much easier than it is in big woods in the East," Maxfield explained. He feels that the first sit of a stand is often the best. "I believe low-budget hunters can be successful because when I hunt a new stand, I'm probably the first guy hunting that area and bucks are often clueless to the stand being there. When I hunt with an outfitter, chances are every stand on the property has been hunted dozens of times. I think [that] finding public or private ground that hasn't been hunted much is fairly easy to do and offers a better opportunity than hunting with an outfitter."

Buying maps in rural states and putting many miles on his truck has helped put dozens of racks on Maxfield's wall.

Michigan's John Eberhart is another hunter who is not afraid to travel. Eberhart has published several books on hunting pressured bucks, and he produced a DVD on the subject. When he is in the mood for an easy hunt, he hunts public and private ground away from home.

"A few years ago, I harvested a massive buck in Illinois on public ground in the late season. I had less than $1,000 invested in the hunt. Everyone believes if you're going to hunt in Illinois, you must go with an outfitter. That is not the case," said Eberhart.

PUTTING THE ODDS IN YOUR FAVOR

Eberhart has been on fourteen self-guided out-of-state whitetail hunts and has tagged twelve bucks. These are amazing odds.

"I start my hunt months in advance by calling the states I plan to hunt in and getting plat books for the area. Before I order the books, I look at topo maps and try to locate rivers and streams near farms. When the crops are cut, the bucks will be concentrated near the river's edge because I have found that is where most of the cover is in many of the farm belt states," Eberhart stated. "After the crops are harvested, the deer are forced into the watershed corridors. Those corridors are where I like to hunt.

PHONE A FRIEND

When Eberhart finds the type of terrain he likes, he uses the plat book to determine who owns the property he wants to hunt and begins making phone calls.

"When I call to order the plat books, I often ask the person on the phone if they know anyone who might let a hunter hunt. A few years ago, a woman gave me the name of a farmer who let me hunt one 80-acre section of his farm in Missouri. I tagged a 160-inch buck on that property. Making many phone calls and asking many questions has helped me become successful over the years. Sometimes farmers say no, but they tell me about some public ground nearby. Every tip helps."

TIMING IS EVERYTHING

Eberhart believes that his success depends on knowing when to hunt and when to stay home.

"One of the main reasons I tag out is because I hunt at the right time. I believe timing is everything," Eberhart explained. "If I go hunting in the middle of October, crops will still be standing. If I go in December, finding the bucks will be harder. By going just before the rut in early or mid-November, I hunt a few days after the crops on most of the farms have been removed, which is when I want to be there. This is when the big bucks are easiest to find, and since I

BIG GAME ON A BUDGET

only have a week to hunt, I need to find them right away."

Eberhart believes many hunters hunt too early in the season, resulting in tougher hunting and poorer results.

Tom Johnson with one of his many bucks he has tagged while hunting on a budget.

PUBLIC LAND POSSIBILITIES

Eberhart says hunters from the South and East shouldn't thumb their noses at public ground.

"In Michigan, most public ground gets over-hunted. Finding big bucks is difficult. In states like Missouri and Kansas, the public ground isn't over-hunted, and you can easily find big bucks that are moving during daylight hours."

Tom Johnson, another hunter from Michigan, has a knack for finding bucks with lots of bone on their heads. Johnson spends considerable time scouting the areas he hunts, and his efforts have paid off; he has tagged several bucks on public land over 150.

SAY CHEESE

One of Johnson's keys to success is locating bucks in areas overlooked by other hunters.

"I spend extensive time scouting and hanging trail cameras to locate bucks on public ground," Johnson explained. "Sometimes a well-placed camera gives me the clues I need to find big bucks."

Johnson often brings three or more cameras on a hunt and does what he calls "speed scouting"—hanging several cameras out at the same time to increase his odds of finding mature bucks

"Over the years, I have learned that big bucks will live anywhere. Sometimes I find them in a small parcel of ground along a highway. Other times I locate them miles from the nearest road, and they are living there because hunters have pushed them deep into the woods."

Johnson has tagged big bucks on his own in Montana, Nebraska, Iowa, and other states on a shoestring budget.

"I love going to new areas and hanging a few cameras to find out what is in the area. Finding big bucks with a camera isn't hard; you just need to know how to read sign and locate deer.

"Out West, it isn't difficult. The deer travel in the little bit of cover there is. Hanging cameras in the cover near travel corridors between bedding areas and feeding areas is often

Using aerial photos and topographical maps is one way to determine where to hang your treestands when hunting in a new place.

the way to find deer. I also hang cameras near a scrape or a rub if it is fresh. Scouting, having lots of time to hunt, and hunting in places where there aren't many hunters has allowed me to tag lots of bucks on public ground."

Johnson is self-employed and believes that having two weeks or more to hunt an area has helped him fill tags over the years.

BIG GAME ON A BUDGET

"Often I tag out as my hunt is ending. It can take weeks for me to figure out an area, and I will move my stands several times if I have to so [that] I am in position to tag a big buck."

BE A CHATTY CATHY

One thing all three of the hunters I talked to have in common is that they aren't afraid to ask questions and knock on doors.

"Locals have taught me more about an area than I could have ever learned on my own in years of hunting," admits Johnson. "Many people still like helping hunters, and by asking the right questions I find myself hunting in some amazing places where there are very few other hunters."

THE LEASE THAT PAID OFF

Johnson's biggest buck came off a piece of property he and a few friends leased in Indiana.

"There are big bucks in Indiana, but I didn't think I would find the kind of buck I shot," Johnson said. "A few friends and I pitched in a few hundred dollars and hunted a farm in Indiana that didn't see much hunting pressure. After bow season ended, all of my friends went elsewhere to hunt. I decided to stay for the opening day of gun season because the guy who oversaw the piece of property we were hunting told me many deer end up on this farm on opening day of gun season because they get pushed onto the property."

Until opening day of gun season, Johnson and his friends had seen a few decent bucks, but no whoppers.

"I wasn't expecting to kill a Booner because we hadn't seen a buck like that on the property, and because it wasn't an enormous farm, but I guess big bucks can live anywhere. On opening day, I shot a buck that scored 218-7/8s. I could see a subdivision and school kids when I shot the buck; proof that you never know where a monster buck is going to be found. The nicest thing about this buck [is] I had less than $1,000 into the hunt," Johnson said with a smile.

All three hunters have a knack for finding big bucks. All three of them scout from home using maps to locate public and private ground that looks like it will hold deer. All of them know that if they want to consistently tag big bucks, they must go where big bucks live because they can't kill big ones in places where bucks can't reach maturity. All three hunters spend a lot of time on the phone asking the right questions, in the field hanging stands, and simply hunting their tails off. As a result, all three tag big bucks almost every year on a shoestring budget.

If you have more elbow grease than money, you, too, can tag a big buck. But like these hunters, plan to sweat a little. Maxfield hangs dozens of treestands each year when scouting and hunting.

Big bucks are a lot of work.

• • • *Checking the Charts* • • •

Do you wonder why hunting whitetails west of the Mississippi River is so much easier than hunting them in the East? Do you wonder why hunters kill so many big bucks in Kansas, Iowa, and Nebraska? Charts published in John Eberhart's book, Precision Bowhunting *tell the tale. The data is from 2001, but I believe it is still accurate.*

The hunter ratio chart clearly shows that many states have 10-20 times fewer bowhunters in the woods than others. This has several positive implications. Fewer hunters mean bucks live longer. Less hunting pressure means fewer hunters are knocking on farmers' doors, and fewer hunters in the woods means bucks aren't hunted as hard, so they are probably easier to pattern and kill.

BIG GAME ON A BUDGET

The author with a bull he shot in Alaska.

3

MOOSE HUNTING

I speak at wild game dinners all across the country, and have discovered from talking to fellow outdoorsman that it is the dream of most diehard hunters to hunt moose. Some fantasize of hunting them in Alaska or the Yukon. Many would settle for hunting them in Maine, Idaho, or Colorado. One thing is certain: moose, regardless of the sub-species, are extremely large and have huge antlers on their head. And that's what makes them popular with hunters.

Moose hunting can be expensive. The average cost of a guided moose hunt in Alaska is between $8,000 and $12,000, sometimes or more. If, however, you have big dreams of chasing moose and a small checking account, realize that with a little research and plenty of effort, you can make your moose hunting dreams come true. I have hunted in Alaska without breaking the bank. To succeed, you must invest as much effort into planning your hunt as you would in the hunting itself.

Moose hunting can be very physically demanding.

Paul Williams of Ohio harvested an Alaskan bull in 2008 and only spent a few thousand dollars on the hunt.

"The most expensive part of my hunt was renting a vehicle," said Williams. "My lodging and meals were inexpensive, and I didn't have the cost of a float plane trip, so my hunt was a low-budget affair."

The main reason Williams' hunt was low-cost was that he hunted moose on Fort Richardson Army Base in Anchorage. Each year the base has a primitive weapon hunt, which allows hunters to use either a muzzleloader or bow. The base offers a fall and an early winter hunt. The toughest thing about the hunt is drawing the tag.

"There isn't a preference point system," said Williams, "so getting drawn is tough. I always wanted to hunt in Alaska, and I figured the Army base hunt would be the least expensive way to hunt moose in Alaska."

Williams was right. Hiring a floatplane service often costs close to two thousand dollars or more.

"Every day I drove to the base and hunted. It was great. No expensive planes or outfitters were needed."

The disadvantage for Williams was that he drew the late-season tag and shot a bull that had lost his antlers.

"My hunt was in December, so some of the bulls were losing their antlers," Williams said. "I didn't want to shoot a cow, and I told my son, who was coming up to hunt with me for a few days in the middle of my hunt, that if I got a shot at a bull I would take it even if he wasn't with me yet."

During one day's hunt, Williams spotted a cow moose and decided to stalk the cow for practice. "As I got closer, I glassed it and saw it was a bull that had lost his antlers. I sat there and wondered what I should do. It was a bull."

Williams decided that if the bull walked out into the open and gave him a broadside shot, he would shoot it. That's exactly what happened.

"I made a good hit on the bull and was very pleased. It was a great experience and I hope to do it again."

Marc Taylor has also hunted moose on Fort Richardson. Taylor now lives in Alaska and owns a Wiggy's Sleeping Bag Store in Anchorage. He has hunted all over the state.

"I have drawn the Fort Richardson moose tag several times, but hunters who want to hunt moose shouldn't plan to get that tag because it is hard to draw," advises Taylor. "They should plan a backcountry trip and do what they can to save money."

Taylor has written several books on hunting in Alaska, and has a book series called *Hunting Hard in Alaska*. He believes that hunters wanting to hunt in Alaska should plan a trip at least a year in advance.

"Alaska is a big place, and hunters looking to come here should start by researching online where to go months in advance, and even buy a book or two on hunting in Alaska," Taylor suggested. "Finding a good flying service to fly them in and drop them off is vital. The chance of getting a bull by walking in from the road is slim. Serious hunters should plan to pay to be flown into the bush. To locate a good fly-in service, do some research. Books and the Alaska Hunting Forum are good places to start. Posting questions about flying services on a forum will often get responded to by hunters who are willing to provide good and bad fly-in companies."

Many of the books published on Alaska hunting actually give locations to where you can be dropped off, what stretches of river to float on, et cetera. Taylor, Larry Bartlett, Michael Strahan, and others have published some great books on the subject.

If you plan to go to Alaska, you need to find the right place to hunt. When looking at a map, remember that some units have antler restrictions and some don't. A few years ago, I hunted moose in Alaska in a unit without an antler restriction, which made hunting more fun because I didn't have to worry whether or not the bull was big enough. In some units, the bulls have to be fifty inches or larger. If you shoot a 49-inch bull, you are in trouble.

When researching areas, calling a biologist is a good way to get information. Dave Battle grew up in North Carolina and moved to Alaska. He regularly called biologists during his first few years in the state.

"Biologists can give you information about the trophy-class potential of the animals in the units they oversee, as well as moose density in their areas, which can help you narrow down your search," Battle explained.

Twelve years ago my dad hunted in Alaska and arrowed a Pope & Young bull on his first day of the hunt. A flying service dropped him and my cousin off on a river system, and within 24 hours they both tagged out. The key to their success was long-distance scouting. My dad called several fly-in services, outfitters, and others he knew in Alaska to locate a good drop-off location and hunting area. Today you only need the Internet to get the same results. Spending time online researching areas, looking at fish and game websites, and talking on forums will easily help you find a good place to hunt. You must act like a detective looking for clues. The more time you have to research and search for clues, the better your hunt will turn out.

If hunting in Alaska on your own isn't something you believe you can do, consider hunting moose in the Lower 48. Many Western states have Shiras Moose. You can also hunt Canadian Moose in Maine. The Yukon Moose in Alaska are the largest, but in the Lower 48, bush planes are not needed, which greatly reduces the cost of the

BIG GAME ON A BUDGET

hunt. If you want to hunt moose in the western states, remember that the tag fees are extreme. A moose tag in Idaho, for example, is over $2,000; however, an Idaho moose hunt would cost less than hunting in Alaska when you consider that an Alaska floatplane trip itself is often $2,000.

If hunting moose in the West sounds like fun, consider buying a subscription to the *Huntin' Fool* magazine. *Huntin' Fool* breaks down the drawing process in all 13 western states, species by species.

Calling in moose can be fun, exciting, and DANGEROUS.

Hunters must draw a tag in order to moose hunt.

"Moose hunting in the West is more reasonable than hunting in Alaska," says Garth Carter of the *Huntin' Fool* magazine. "In some units, getting drawn isn't going to take years. There are some units in Idaho that have leftover tags."

Regardless of the location of the moose hunt, the process will test you physically and mentally, especially if you are doing everything yourself without the help of an outfitter.

"Quartering up a moose and packing it out is a lot of work," Marc Taylor cautions. "Hunters need to be in shape if they come to hunt moose. Having good gear is also important. The weather can be extreme in the West and in Alaska. Having a top-notch sleeping bag, tent, and backpack are key."

Taylor and many hunters who spend significant time in the backcountry use lightweight tipis that come with a collapsible wood stove. I use a Kifaru tipi. Taylor uses a similar unit made by Titanium Goat.

Most moose hunting takes place in the bush, which requires a ride in a float plane.

"A lightweight tipi is durable and packs into a small bag, which is important when packing in," says Taylor. "When flying in somewhere, you need lightweight gear because float planes have weight restrictions."

Moose are not the brightest light bulbs in the closet. They will often walk within bow range of a bowhunter if the hunter is a decent caller.

"In the rut, a bull will come running up to the sound of a cow moan, which makes moose a bowhunter's dream come true," Taylor claims. When Taylor says bull moose will get close, he means it. My dad's moose walked within eight yards of him after Dad spent a few minutes of brushing trees with a stick and grunting like a bull.

If you are a hunter on a budget like me, the best way to hunt several big game animals is by putting in for tags. Whether you plan to hunt in Alaska, Maine, or Idaho, if you draw a limited-draw tag, your chances of going on a low-budget hunt and tagging a big bull increase dramatically. The possibility of drawing a Fort Richardson moose tag is less than five percent, but if you draw, you have the equivalent of a Wal-Mart moose hunt. If you don't put in for the Fort Richardson tag because the odds of getting it are small, your chances of getting a bull are zero.

"I have drawn that tag four times, which is crazy when you consider the odds," said Taylor. "I have shot some great bulls; one that was 58 inches wide."

While you are applying for a tag in Alaska, put in for Western moose tags and Maine moose tags at the same time. Eventually, you will get lucky. In Maine, you can buy extra draws, which increases your odds.

My 2008 moose hunt cost about $2,500. My dad's was $3,500 in 1997. Paul Williams said he had less than $3,000 in his hunt. If you pinch pennies, even with the cost of flying into the bush, you can hunt moose for less than $4,000 in Alaska, and even less in the Lower 48. If you want to save money, get an Alaska Airline credit card. I put everything I buy on this card and earn free airline tickets. I have hunted and fished in Alaska twice in the last two years. I have never paid for my airfare, which saved me between $800 and $1,000 on each trip.

If you want to hunt moose, do lots of research, get in shape, and practice your calling. You may find yourself staring at a bull moose at eight yards.

Tracy Breen

The author with a backcountry bull he killed in New Mexico.

4

ELK ON A SHOESTRING

Every hardcore whitetail hunter I know dreams of going on a Western elk hunt. Many hunters believe an out-of-state elk hunt is beyond their financial reach. After all, if you look online at elk hunting outfitters, you will realize that going on a guided elk hunt can set you back $4,000 or more. I have been on guided elk hunts that cost as much as $10,000. That said, don't let those high-price hunts scare you. By doing a little homework, saving your pennies, and getting into shape, going on an unguided do-it-yourself elk hunt is within anyone's price range. In the last decade, I have gone on several elk hunts that cost less than $1,500. And you can, too!

If you plan to go on an elk hunt in a state far away like Colorado,

Idaho, or New Mexico (that's assuming you live east of the Mississippi), try to plan your trips months or even a year in advance. Order topographical maps to locate good hunting areas, call game biologists in the area you plan to hunt, and research and buy top-notch gear so you are ready for a backcountry-style adventure.

I plan to be away from home for at least fourteen days when I elk hunt. Many hunters gasp when I say this, like they are about to hold their breath and go for a swim underwater, but the more time you have in the field, the better chance you have of tagging an animal. Hunting in unfamiliar territory has a steep learning curve. If you haven't been elk hunting or haven't been elk hunting on your own, figuring out where the elk live, feed, and bed can take several days or weeks. If you take a week off work and subtract travel time, you have only four or five days to hunt.

Packing out meat is rewarding and exhausting.

It can take that long to locate elk. Many hunters go home empty-handed because they run out of time. Time is the most important tool when it comes to being a successful elk hunter.

If you have time on your hands, you will be able to locate and pattern elk. You will even be able to mess up a time or two (which often happens to first-time elk hunters and veterans alike) and still have plenty of time to connect with an animal. In 2009, a friend and I each drew a New Mexico bull elk tag for a coveted unit. We were gone from home for eighteen days. Our season was less than ten days, but we scouted hard for four or five days before our season opened. We questioned our sanity after ten days in the field without

BIG GAME ON A BUDGET

a shower and a good meal, but when we both came home proudly carrying a set of elk horns, being physically exhausted and dirty was a distant memory.

When elk hunting on your own, the best way to find elk is often by breaking in a pair of boots and hunting miles of roadless areas. Whether you are hunting deer in the East or elk in the West, one thing is consistent: most hunters are lazy and don't want to travel any farther from camp and the pickup truck than they have to. Finding elk often requires extensive walking and glassing.

One of the best methods of locating elk is by hunting and staying off the beaten path. Many hunters prefer having a base camp that they return to each night. I like keeping my food, shelter, and gear on my back and camping where I end the days' hunt. This can save time and keeps me in the wilderness 24 hours a day. Many hunters spend the last hour of light heading back to camp, yet the first and last hours of daylight are often the most productive. By living in the woods among the elk, patterning them and listening to them, I gain many clues as to where the elk are spending their time.

Having a top-notch backpack is a must when elk hunting.

One great scouting trick that works well if you are camping in the wilderness is staying up several hours after dark or getting up several hours before daylight and listening to the bulls bugle. Like a tom turkey that quits gobbling to hen yelps during turkey season, a bull elk often quits bugling in the fall when hunters bugle at him. They bugle after dark when they feel they are alone. I have located several herds over the years by staying up listening to elk. After the elk are located, I try to figure out where they bed and feed. Elk often feed until midmorning and then head for a bedding area. If I know where they are spending the night, I can try to cut them off on the way to the bedding area without blowing on a bugle tube.

The payoff..hundreds of pounds of meat.

When hunting elk in the backcountry or on your own, one of your most valuable tools is a GPS that you know how to use. Let me say that again: having a GPS you know how to use. Many hunters pick up a GPS at Cabela's on their way to a hunt and learn how to use it while they are hunting. On my New Mexico elk hunt, I used a Lowrance Ihunt C GPS that had topographical maps of the unit I was hunting downloaded onto it. When I showed up in New Mexico, I understood how to use my GPS. I also recognized the water tanks, logging roads, mountains, and ridges that were labeled on it, so it was like having a cheat sheet. My friend, Tom, and I checked out several water tanks and logging roads for elk sign before our hunt started. We narrowed down our options long before we started hunting. When our season opened, we used the GPS to get back to our hotspots that we marked, and to navigate around in the backcountry without getting lost. I also carried a small Bushnell Backtrack GPS and compass so that when we headed into the backcountry, we wouldn't have to worry about getting lost. When you're not worried about getting lost, you hunt harder and longer, which often results in a higher success rate.

Heading to a place you have never been before and wandering around in the wilderness with nothing more than a map, GPS, and

BIG GAME ON A BUDGET

some gear on your back can be intimidating for Eastern whitetail hunters. I believe whitetail hunters should hunt elk like they hunt deer. Buy a good topographical map for the unit you are hunting in months before leaving home. Try to locate water holes and backcountry streams where elk would likely drink. Bring a treestand with you on your hunt and hang it in a large tree near that waterhole.

In addition to bringing a treestand, pack a scouting camera. Elk often water at the same waterhole each day. If you can locate such a waterhole and hang a scouting camera over it, it won't take long for you to figure out what time of day the elk are visiting the waterhole and you will know when to be there. By the way, elk rarely are hunted from a treestand, so they don't look up like whitetails. Hunting from a treestand over water in the West can be like hunting deer over a corn feeder. It can be very easy.

The author and his hunting buddy Tom with Tom's bull he killed on public land in 2014. This do-it-yourself bull didn't break the bank and it had over 350 inches of antler on its head.

Put a whitetail hunter in a section of woods with elk in it and, eventually, the hunter will find the elk. One of the reasons the success rate on public land elk hunting is so low is because many hunters don't find the elk. Colorado is a big place. Finding good places to hunt can be a daunting task. Start your search by going online and looking for information. I've had great luck calling and talking with game biologists. They won't give you their favorite honey hole, but they might tell you which units are hunted hardest and which units are overlooked by hunters. My favorite question to ask is what unit is extremely rugged that most hunters won't venture into. That's where I want to hunt. Find remote areas that receive little hunting pressure and you will probably find elk. Another option is subscribing to a magazine called *Huntin' Fool*. This magazine breaks down the best elk hunting units in the West. *Western Hunter* magazine also does this.

There is something about wandering around in the mountains, listening to elk bugle, that calls this flatlander back West almost every year. Elk hunting is physically and mentally exhausting. It is not unusual for me to lose fifteen pounds or more on a two-week hunt, but when I am sitting on my couch months after a hunt, the pain and agony of the hunt are gone, I can relive the happy memories that will last a lifetime.

A drop-camp often includes a horse packer who will pack out your bull after the kill.

5

FULLY GUIDED VS. DROP-CAMP HUNTING

There are many ways to hunt Western elk. You can go on an unguided hunt, a guided hunt, or you can go on a drop-camp hunt. Most first-time elk hunters choose one of the latter two options.

One of the main reasons elk hunters decide to go on a guided hunt or a drop-camp hunt versus an unguided hunt is because the success rate of an unguided hunt hovers around ten percent. To put that in perspective, if one hundred hunters go on an elk hunt, only ten come home with meat. Of the ten animals killed, less than half are going to be bulls. Therefore, if killing a bull elk is on your bucket list, it is probably in your best interest to go on a guided elk hunt of some type.

FIVE STAR ELK HUNTS

First, let's discuss fully guided elk hunts.

There are high-end guided hunts, low-end guided hunts, and middle-of-the-road guided hunts. In my experience, the more you pay, the higher your chance of success.

Several years ago, I went on a high-end elk hunt at Three Forks Ranch in Northern Colorado. From the moment I arrived, I expected Robin Leach to step out from one of the luxury cabins and greet me. The place is that fancy. When most people think about elk hunting, they imagine roughing it in a tent. Three Forks Ranch is far from roughing it. I stayed in a million dollar log home and ate like a king.

The accommodations at Three Forks Ranch is a far cry from a wall tent.

A few of the hunters even brought their non-hunting wives along to enjoy the experience.

The elk hunting was equally amazing. The private ranch is home to thousands of free-ranging elk.

"We guess that we have about 7,000 or more elk here in the fall, so it is safe to say that anyone who comes here to elk hunt is going to see elk and hear many bugling bulls," said Justin Flaherty, Manager of the Ranch. "Three Forks offers five-day hunts for bowhunters and gun hunters. Like most hunting operations, they offer 2x1 guided hunts and 1x1 guided hunts. Either way, every hunter who comes to Three Forks Ranch gets a shot at an elk. We don't have a 100-percent success rate because sometimes things go wrong, so some hunters go home empty-handed. We do have a 100-percent opportunity rate on a 5x5 bull or better."

These are amazing odds, especially for bowhunters, but it is true. I witnessed it first-hand. The year I bowhunted at Three Forks Ranch, every bowhunter went home with a bull or had an opportunity to shoot one.

One reason the hunting is superb is that all the hunting takes place on private land.

"Three Forks Ranch is made up of 200,000 acres of land," said Flaherty. "The hunting takes place on 50,000 acres."

As a result, there is very little hunting pressure. On my first day of hunting at Three Forks Ranch, I must have heard a hundred different bulls bugle. I personally laid eyes on hundreds of elk, including one decent Pope and Young bull.

How much does an elk hunt cost at Three Forks Ranch? It is about $9,000 for a five-day hunt. This price will cause many of you to almost faint, but with five-star accommodations that rival any New York City eatery and a nearly 100-percent success rate, they can charge that much. Remember that once you arrive at Three Forks, you will never open your wallet until it is time to have meat processed or a trophy mounted. "When we say our hunts are all-inclusive, we mean it," said Flaherty. "The food, the drinks, and all the extras are included. Hunters don't even tip their guides."

BLUE COLLAR ELK HUNTS

Fortunately, the Three Forks Ranch price range isn't the price all outfitters charge for an elk hunt. Cache Creek Outfitters, also in Colorado, charges $3,500 to $4,000 for a five-day guided hunt, and the opportunity rate on these hunts averages 60-70 percent regardless of weapons. About 30 to 40 percent of bowhunters go home with a bull.

"We hunt public land in Colorado," says Jeff Miner, owner of Cache Creek. "We have private land hunts in New Mexico, but the prices are a bit higher. We offer fully guided hunts where hunters stay in a cabin every night, and off-the-beaten path wall tent hunts where hunters hunt from horseback. Some hunters prefer the extreme wilderness experience, so we have something to suit everyone."

Included in the price is 2x1 guiding and all the meals, field dressing, and removing the animal from the backcountry. Regardless, if you choose to go on the high-end hunt or the middle-of-the-road when you go on a guided hunt, the main thing you are paying for is the knowledge of the outfitter and the guide. That knowledge is what puts the odds in your favor.

"Our guides spend a lot of time in the woods and know where the elk live, which is important. We know where they are at in the early season and in the rut," Miner said.

DROP-CAMPS

If a guided hunt is out of your price range, or you simply want to hunt on your own but want the knowledge of a guide at your fingertips, you may consider going on a drop-camp hunt. The cost of a drop-camp hunt with Cache Creek is $1,750. They provide a tent, a stove, and a few amenities, bring you into the camp, and pack out the elk for you. The hunting and most of the work is on your shoulders.

"Some hunters enjoy hunting on their own with their buddies and calling for themselves. These types of hunters are independent and like roughing it," says Miner.

Many hunters choose this style of hunt because it is half the price of a guided hunt. Keep in mind if this style of hunt appeals to you, you will need to be prepared to live in the backcountry and all that accompanies it.

"Some bowhunters like the idea of hunting in the backcountry by themselves, but aren't really prepared for it physically and mentally."

If you plan to hunt in a drop-camp, get yourself into shape, be comfortable using a compass and GPS, and be sure you know how to field-dress an animal.

The success rate on drop-camp hunts is often much lower than guided hunts. The success rate at Cache Creek is often around 25 to 30 percent. This may sound like low odds, but keep in mind the overall success rate in Colorado is ten percent with a bow, so if you go on a drop-camp hunt, your odds are two to three times as high as they would be if you went on your own.

MANY OPTIONS

It is sometimes hard to know which type of hunt is best for your situation. You should factor in a few things when deciding what type of hunt to choose. If you are planning to go on an elk hunt once in your life, go on a guided elk hunt. If your wife wants to experience the West, consider going to a ranch like Three Forks Ranch. If you think you might only elk hunt twice, I would suggest going on a guided hunt both times. Chances are, if you go on two guided elk hunts, you will come home with a bull at least once. If you want a large bull, I suggest going with an outfitter. Your chances of killing a 300-inch bull (or bigger) are much greater with an outfitter than without. Remember that the average bull taken with a large percentage of outfitters is probably in the 250-inch to 280-inch range—a nice bull, especially with a bow.

Most drop camps include the use of a nice wall tent.

If elk hunting is something that you would like to do five or ten times in your life and you are fairly independent, I would start by going on a drop-camp hunt and learning the ropes of Western hunting in the backcountry. After experiencing that style of hunting and getting your feet wet, you can branch out and start hunting on your own.

• • • *The Guide Knows Best* • • •

Matt Guedes is a guide for Cache Creek Outfitters and has personally hunted all over the world on guided hunts. He says if someone wants to be successful on an elk hunt, regardless of whether they go on a fully guided trip or a drop-camp hunt, they need to listen to their guide or outfitter.

"Over the years, I have guided many hunters who are good bowhunters," says Guedes. "When they get out here, they try to use the knowledge they have gained in the whitetail woods on elk, often ignoring the advice of their guide. A guide often puts the hunter in a certain spot or setup based on years of experience. When hunters second-guess their guide and go off on their own or try to hunt their own way, they often go home without a bull. I'm not saying we know everything about hunting, but I'm saying a hunter should work with his guide. As a team, the chances of success are much higher."

• • • *Save Your Pennies* • • •

Elk hunting is in almost everyone's price range. Over the years, I have gone on guided elk hunts and unguided elk hunts and have harvested elk both ways. Since bowhunting is a priority for me, I save so I can afford to hunt. I don't drive a new truck or buy fancy clothes. I make sacrifices so I can go elk hunting. If elk hunting sounds like something you would like to do, save your pennies and go. You will enjoy a trip you will never forget.

• • • *No Electronics* • • •

If you are an Eastern hunter heading west for the first time, be aware that most Western states do not allow any electronic devices on your bow or arrow. Rangefinders attached to the bow, sights that have a light for seeing in low light conditions, and lighted nocks are against the law. If you really like using lighted nocks, there are a couple alternatives. Norway Industries makes the Zeon Vane, which is a vane that gathers light and is extremely bright in low-light conditions. Flex Fletch makes glow-in-the-dark vanes that work well.

BIG GAME ON A BUDGET

• • • *Where Did the Air Go?* • • •

If you are a flatlander heading west, realize that the air is thinner out West, which can make you miserable. Many hunters get altitude sickness—a condition that causes fatigue and vomiting, often causing hunters to go to a lower elevation. One way to reduce the chance of this happening is by taking a pill called Altitude Advantage. This product is made by Wilderness Athlete, and it helps your body process oxygen faster at high altitude. Your doctor can also prescribe medication to solve the problem.

Tracy Breen

Tom Johnson with his Wyoming bull.

6

PERSISTENCE PAYS

Tom Johnson has spent the last thirty-one years chasing elk out West. Although he lives in West Michigan, he sleeps and breathes elk hunting. He is a true "elk-oholic." In those thirty-one years, he has tagged two bulls with his bow.

You're about to read an amazing story of one man's persistence, strong will, and ability to stay focused on a goal.

If the Yankees had two wins and thirty-one losses, most of America would give up hope on them. If the Detroit Red Wings made it to the finals thirty-one times and choked twenty-nine times, most people would make fun of them and assume they weren't good enough to win anymore. Johnson, on the other hand, is good enough.

Johnson has chased elk almost every year for thirty-one years with a bow in his hand. Johnson is an accomplished hunter. If you walk into his office, you will quickly notice more Pope & Young bucks on the wall than most hunters tag in a lifetime. Johnson tagged every one of them the hard way—by hunting on his own—mainly on public land in states across the country. Although his office and house are full of bone, one thing you wouldn't have seen until a few years ago was a large bull elk. You would see a moose rack from Alaska, Caribou mounts, and Dall Sheep, but the bow-killed elk was missing from the lineup.

Johnson has what many call Iron Bull Syndrome. In case you are unfamiliar with this condition, it is an illness that often strikes the moment a large bull walks into view when you are holding a bow in your hand. You start sweating, get nervous, and lose your ability to think straight. The illness only affects Johnson when he is chasing bull elk; no other species causes the problem.

"Shortly after I got married thirty-one years ago, a friend, Bob, and I went elk hunting in Colorado," said Johnson. "Bob lived in Denver, and neither of us knew how to elk hunt. We did the hunt inexpensively. We slept in the back of a truck and hunted hard. We stopped and bought little elk whistles meant to imitate the bugle of a bull, but they sounded more like a play toy. However, they worked."

On one of the first days of the hunt, Johnson and his friend heard a bull bugle about a mile away. They blew into their whistle.

"He bugled back at our calls but he wouldn't move. We wondered why he wouldn't come in. He was a mile away. That was the reason!" Johnson laughed.

The next day the bull bugled in the same place and this time Johnson went after him.

"We shortened the distance between the bull and us. We were probably seven hundred yards away when we called to him and he responded. We worked our way towards him and got set up and he

BIG GAME ON A BUDGET

started coming in. He came in to that little whistle bugle."

The bull eventually stepped out of some aspens about thirty-five yards from Johnson. He was a big, mature 6x6 bull. Johnson drew his bow and let an arrow fly.

"I don't remember aiming that first shot. The arrow hit a tree! The bull stood there, so I let another arrow fly and whack! I hit the tree a few inches below the first arrow."

Johnson shot a couple more times at the bull and at one point took many hairs off the bulls' belly with one of the shots.

"I didn't wound him; I just got a little hair. I never got the bull."

That bull remained etched in Johnson's mind for decades. Over the next thirty years, Johnson became a professional at taking hair off the bellies of bulls and cows.

"The amazing thing is that I have shot at over a dozen elk and haven't wounded one badly. I always shot over them, under them, behind them, or in front of them, for the most part."

As the years passed, Johnson started taking elk hunting seriously, just as he does deer hunting.

"I've hunted some good areas out West. I have applied for tags and drew some great tags, but something always went wrong at the moment of truth," Johnson explained.

Once, when Johnson was hunting in Colorado, he called in a 5x5 up close and personal. Things were going well.

"I called this bull in and stopped him where I wanted him with a call or two. I thought it was a slam dunk shot. However, I watched in disbelief as the arrow went right over the top of his back. I just couldn't hold it together."

The next day, Johnson missed another bull.

As the years went by, Johnson got frustrated but became more determined.

"I know one of the big reasons I struggled is because I don't live near elk, so the only time I see them is a few days a year when I am hunting them. The moment I see them I get flipped out. I really got frustrated with myself when year in and year out I brought friends with me on archery elk hunts and they killed an elk on their first trip out West. It made me that much more determined to tag a bull."

When some people get skunked year after year, they get frustrated and give up. The longer Johnson went without putting an arrow in a bull, he thought about elk more, did more research on elk hunting, and fine-tuned his archery skills.

In 2007, after nearly thirty years of going home empty-handed, Johnson's luck changed.

"I drew a tag in Wyoming in a trophy unit that holds large bulls. On this hunt, I helped a friend get a 340-class bull, so we were all in good spirits. My friend tagged his bull by spot and stalking it. We were really starting to figure out how to spot and stalk elk and not call," Johnson recalled.

A day or two after the 340-class bull went down, Johnson and a friend were staying close with a herd of elk in hopes that one of the bulls would lag behind the herd and they could slip in on it and get a shot.

"Things were going well that day. We had a decent bull in close. We weren't calling; we were stalking, and eventually we got close to a big bull, but the bull saw my friend and bolted."

With no better options, Johnson stayed after the spooked bull, but eventually the bull was too far in front of him to catch up. In the process of chasing the spooked bull, Johnson heard a low growl.

"It sounded more like a moo cow than an elk, but we decided we should go investigate. The sounds we heard were crazy, so we went trucking in that direction. We didn't expect to find a bull, but when we walked into a clearing, we saw a big bull in the brush raking trees about seventy yards away. It was a gift from God after all those years!"

Without much time to think, Johnson started walking fast across the opening towards the bull. The bull was busy raking branches and didn't notice Johnson slipping in on him like a hungry mountain lion. "The bull was destroying the branches and was wedged between the trees. I stopped and came to full draw at about twenty-five yards. When I came to full draw, the bull noticed me, looked over his shoulder at me, and started to quickly get out of the trees. I made a noise and he stopped to look at me. I tried to aim and let the arrow fly," Johnson said.

Like many times before, Johnson was shaking like a leaf, but this time the outcome was different. The arrow hit his spine and the bull collapsed. The bull scored 319.

Once the monkey was off Johnson's back, everything changed. In 2009, Johnson and I hunted 16D in New Mexico. Unlike many of Johnson's hunts, the New Mexico hunt turned out great. Towards

Tom prefers staying in a camper when elk hunting. He often has a base camp, as shown, and a spike camp that consists of a tent miles from his RV.

the end of our hunt, with my bull already tagged and cut up, Johnson slipped in on a large bull and put an arrow in him at forty-eight yards. The bull only went ten or twenty yards after the shot before piling up.

Now that Johnson has two bulls on his wall, his confidence is up. With another elk hunt planned for next fall, he is ready for the task.

"It has taken me years to figure out this elk hunting game, but I wouldn't change much even if I could. All the hunts that led up to my Wyoming hunt were fun and I learned a lot. Now I am all about spot-and-stalk hunting and don't spend much time calling. Elk hunting is a lot of work and lots of fun!"

Elk hunting is all about hard work and perseverance. Johnson excels at both. I've hunted with many people over the years. He is one of the few I have hunted with that is willing to go the extra mile (literally) in the planning stages of a hunt and while hunting to ensure he gets into animals on every hunt.

Johnson is also very budget-minded. If you think you have to be rich to elk hunt, remember that most of Johnson's hunts have set him back less than $1,000. If you are mentally tough and willing to endure years of dry spells, maybe you can find success in the backcountry, just like Johnson.

Hunting is not always just about antlers and success. It is also about the sometimes long journey that eventually leads you to success. After thirty-one years and over a dozen missed shots on elk, Johnson has finally tagged several bulls. It wouldn't be much of a story if he would have given up after all those years. If you want to tag monster bulls, you must be mentally tough and have an understanding spouse.

• • • *Time* • • •

If you are planning a public land hunt for elk, realize that time in the woods is often the key to success. Johnson often hunts twelve to eighteen days when elk hunting or when he goes on out-of-state whitetail hunts. Having that kind of time allows him to scout, find animals, connect the dots, and put trophies on the wall. Are you planning a do-it-yourself hunt? If you can spend at least ten days in the woods and take at least two weeks away from home, your chances of success will likely go way up.

BIG GAME ON A BUDGET

The author packing out a caribou rack.

7

CARIBOU HUNTING

Hunting is often a low-percentage proposition. If you go deer hunting and hope to harvest a record book buck, it will probably take you years to achieve your dream. If you go elk hunting with hopes of killing a monster bull, you will probably hunt them for years before you get that lucky. The same can be said for most big game animals, except caribou.

Herds of caribou often include thousands of animals. If you hunt hard for five or ten days, you will likely harvest a bull before going home. Most Canadian and Alaskan outfitters who offer caribou hunts almost guarantee success. In many cases, they guarantee two caribou bulls. A few years ago, I hunted with Luco Caribou Adventures in Quebec, and in five days of hunting, my father-in-law and I harvested three caribou. The success rate on caribou hunts often exceeds 90 percent in most Canadian provinces and in Alaska.

One of the best things about caribou hunting is it takes place in remote country that can only be reached by bush plane. Flying over the Canadian tundra, staring down at the thousands of lakes below, is a sight I will never forget. In addition, I saw caribou runways scratched into the tundra by caribou using the same path for hundreds of years.

After our pilot dropped us off in the bush, our home was a cabin that consisted of canvas and plywood. It didn't look like much, but it kept the rain off our heads and the hot wood stove kept us warm and cozy after long days of hunting.

Caribou hunting isn't like any other type of hunting. You don't sit in treestands for long hours, call them in, or hunt them on the edge of food plots or corn fields. When caribou hunting, you glass for hours until you find them. For the most part, caribou follow the same travel routes year after year and migrate from spring and summer calving and feeding grounds to fall and winter grounds, eating as they go. Most outfitters place hunters near typical migration routes, and the hunters glass for caribou, waiting until they pass within range of their bow or gun.

One of the best places to sit and wait for caribou is near a water crossing.

"Often caribou will travel to a certain spot along a lake edge and cross the lake, heading to their wintering grounds," John Engelken, Caribou Guide for Luco Caribou Adventures, explains. "I often place hunters near the water's edge by the crossing locations, hoping that the caribou will cross by the hunter. Year after year, caribou often cross large lakes in the same places. I have certain spots that have been very productive for hunters."

It is not uncommon to spot herds of several hundred or several thousand when caribou hunting. On my caribou hunt, we hunted for five days without laying eyes on a caribou. The sixth day, however, was a different story. Over two hours, we saw thousands of caribou, and that's when I tagged mine.

Observing thousands of caribou cross in front of you in single file is a great sight to see, but not always ideal, according to Engelken.

"When hunting, I believe seeing several small herds of caribou during a week can result in better hunting than seeing several thousand in one day. When you are able to see several small bands of caribou during a hunt, you have the opportunity to sort of choose the caribou you want to harvest. When you see thousands of them

A large floatplane is often the only way in and out of caribou camp. Most hunters never forget the fly in experience.

in one shot, you have to take advantage of the situation and shoot quickly."

On my hunt, from the moment I saw the caribou until we tagged our bulls was less than an hour. One of the neatest things I've seen in my life occurred after I tagged my bull. As we made the miles hike back to our boat, we bumped into several herds of caribou. At one point, I had large bulls within forty yards of me. I put my caribou rack on my head and walked towards them. They stopped and stared at me, not knowing if I was a caribou or some crazy creature they had never seen before.

Caribou hunting is an amazing adventure!

If you plan on going on a caribou hunt, get yourself into the best shape of your life. Although in most cases you will have a guide with you, you'll need to pack out much of your own meat.

When I hunted in Quebec, we harvested three caribou in fifteen minutes, so we had lots of meat to pack back to the boat. My father-in-law, who accompanied me on this hunt, had 125 pounds of meat in his pack when we left the kill site. We know this because we weighed his pack when we returned to camp. He packed that meat

Caribou camp is often made up of comfortable shacks made of plywood and canvas.

several miles back to the boat.

In addition to being in good shape, having top-notch gear is vital. It's likely that you'll do plenty of walking when hunting, so having good hunting boots can make your hunt much more enjoyable. If you use cheap boots, your ankles can roll when walking on the tundra or you can get lots of blisters. In both cases, your dream hunt could turn into a disaster if you don't have good waterproof boots.

Having a good backpack is also important. You will likely pack out meat that can weigh over 100 pounds. Although that sounds like a lot, if you have a good backpack, one hundred pounds can feel like fifty pounds. On the other hand, if you buy a cheap backpack that doesn't fit right, one hundred pounds can feel like two hundred pounds. Some hunters prefer a backpack with an external aluminum frame, while others prefer a pack with an internal frame. Try on a few packs before deciding which type you prefer.

Some hunters prefer to hunt caribou with a gun while others prefer a bow. Both weapons can quickly bring down a caribou. If you are a bowhunter, practice shooting at long ranges. Forty or fifty-yard shots are not unusual in caribou country. You're often hunting in open terrain, where stalking can be difficult. The longer the shot you feel comfortable taking, the better chance you have of getting a caribou or two. Although caribou look large, your whitetail bow will probably get the job done.

When I hunted caribou, my broadhead and arrow combination was slightly less than 400 grains. I also use this arrow setup for deer and elk.

If you plan on caribou hunting with a gun, use the firearm you feel comfortable shooting. The most common gun used for caribou is a .30-06 because it's what many deer hunters use. My father-in-law brought a .270, and it quickly killed caribou.

You might think you need to take long shots with a gun when caribou hunting, but in most cases you won't have to shoot beyond 100-150 yards, which most whitetail hunters can easily make. Any basic 3-9x40 scope will get the job done.

If you don't want to hunt caribou with an outfitter, hunt in Alaska. They allow nonresidents to hunt caribou without a guide. You can hire a bush plane to drop you into the middle of the tundra in a known caribou hang out, or you can hunt from the Haul Road outside of Fairbanks. The Haul Road is the only place in Alaska you can hunt caribou without having to leave the road system. The road follows the oil pipeline, and you can often see caribou on the tundra from your vehicle. If you want to bowhunt, you can park your vehicle and start hunting. If you want to gun hunt, you have to be at least five miles off the road. Many bowhunters who hunt the Haul Road report having to take sixty-eighty yard shots in the wind. If hunting the Haul Road sounds like fun, practice shooting your bow!

When caribou hunting, the most important thing to bring with you is your patience. You are at the mercy of the caribou. If the caribou migration hasn't reached where you are hunting, you must wait for them. Unlike deer hunting, you can't get up and drive to a new spot or hike over the next ridge. It doesn't work that way. I hunted five days before seeing a caribou. We glassed for hours and hiked all over the place. Eventually the caribou showed up.

Also, the planes fly when the weather is right. If there is a lot wind, rain, or snow, you might not fly in or out the day you were planning. Caribou hunting teaches you to roll with the punches. It doesn't matter if you have to be at work on Monday or if you want to kill a caribou. Everything in the bush is on a different schedule than ours. The planes fly when they can and the caribou migrate when and where they want.

The author with a caribou he killed in Quebec.

If you are looking for a wilderness adventure where you can walk in places rarely touched by man and see wildlife galore, go on a caribou hunt. It will be a trip you won't forget, and you will probably come home with a mind full of great memories, a rack or two for the wall, and a freezer full of fresh caribou meat.

The author with a Texas hog. Hunting hogs is fun and inexpensive.

8

HOG HUNTING IN TEXAS

Anyone who wants a fun hunt they will never forget should go after wild hogs. Sure, a pig doesn't have antlers, most of them aren't that big, and they are all ugly, but hunting pigs is a lot of fun and can be addictive. I have hunted moose in Alaska, caribou in Quebec, and elk all over the West. Visiting these far off places is fun, but it costs a lot more than chasing hogs. Hunting for hogs, on the other hand, costs very little and is as fun as chasing big game animals. If killing a few pigs sounds exciting, pack your bags and head for Texas.

One of the biggest problems associated with most big game hunting is it is a low percentage game. The success rate with elk hunting in Colorado with archery gear hovers around ten percent. Whitetail hunting in Illinois is about 30 percent. Hog hunting in Texas is a different story. If you can hit the broadside of a barn, you will likely kill as many hogs as you can fit in a cooler, or several coolers. When you make a mistake and blow a shot, there are thousands more hogs available, meaning another opportunity is likely around the next cactus!

Many people will tell you that if you want to be a good hunter you have to learn from the school of hard knocks. I think the school of hard knocks is a good teacher, but success is one of the best teachers you will ever find. When you do something right, the light bulb goes off in your head and you know how to do it again. Hog hunting has helped me bring my hunting skills to the next level.

If you have problems with buck fever, if you need to hone your stalking skills, or if your freezer is empty, hog hunting is for you. Most of us have struggled with buck fever in the past. Shooting at a square target in the backyard is a lot different than shooting at a live creature. Most hunters can easily group arrows the size of a pie plate or smaller when shooting in the backyard, but that changes when the buck is standing broadside at 25 yards. A feral hog is not a Pope & Young whitetail, but it is a living animal that requires you to focus and aim properly in order to quickly harvest it. In fact, a hog can be as challenging to hunt as a whitetail.

I hunted at the Dos Plumas Ranch in Texas one February. This ranch gets hunted almost 365 days a year. To say the hogs are a little skittish is an understatement. While hunting, several hogs busted me. They use the wind like whitetails. They don't start moving until just before dark, like whitetails, and if hunters make even the slightest noise, they are in the next county before you can say "bacon."

The average hog weighs around 100 pounds, making them small targets. The vitals on a hog are far forward and very low, creating a challenging target because their shoulder blade is tough to penetrate. Add the fact that they don't bleed very well (I'm sorry to say, but the saying "bleeds like a stuck pig" is a fallacy) and you have an animal that is difficult to harvest. Since every ranch in Texas is covered in hogs, and since their bellies rule hogs, if hunters hunt hard for a number of days, they will eventually score and have a full cooler.

The first day of my four-day hunt, I came up empty-handed and started to worry. The pigs were much smarter than I gave them credit. I didn't see a pig until it was too dark to shoot. The next morning I stalked several small herds of pigs and they busted me. The second evening I scored on a small hog that ended up tasting delicious.

On the third morning of the hunt, Texas got a blanket of fresh snow, which made finding fresh tracks and stalking hogs quite easy. Getting a shot, on the other hand, wasn't. I spent two hours within twenty yards of a group of hogs, waiting for one to make a mistake. Three different hogs were within steps of getting shot, only to spot me at the last second. When you put fifteen or twenty hogs together, getting within bow range and getting a shot off is difficult when forty eyes are always on the alert. I didn't get a pig on this morning, either, but since I am from the Midwest and grew up hunting from treestands, I have little experience stalking game. I enjoyed stalking hogs. Learning to be extremely quiet when I walk, playing the wind, and being patient for what seemed like days are skills that don't come easy. These pigs helped me hone my stalking skills.

During the next several days, I shot two more hogs. On my four-day hunt, I put three hogs in the freezer, which brings me to my next point.

Pork.

Pork tastes great, whether you purchase it at the supermarket or take it from a ranch, and my wife agrees. I packed seventy pounds of meat in a cooler when I finished hunting and flew home. That pork has been some of the best meat I have ever brought home and some of the least expensive. Pork is a meat many hunters enjoy. There are a variety of ways to cook it, which is one reason many people travel to Texas annually to hog hunt. A friend of mine who drove to Texas from New York brought home almost 200 pounds of pork from this trip. His family ate like royalty for a year.

The nicest thing about hunting in Texas is the cost. Elk can cost you thousands of dollars to hunt, as will trophy deer. Hogs at the Dos Plumas Ranch will set you back about $125 a day, which includes lodging. When you look at the cost of the hunt versus buying pork in the store, it is often about the same, especially when you bring home mostly tenderloin, as I did.

Alan Williams, owner of the Dos Plumas Ranch, called his place the working man's ranch.

"When I started this ranch, my main goal was to create a place where the average Joe could go and enjoy himself, harvest a few animals, and not break the bank doing it," Williams said.

A four or five-day package at many of the ranches in Texas will cost less than $1,000, and you will get many opportunities to harvest hogs. You'll also have the time of your life.

There are many options if hog hunting sounds like fun to you. At the Dos Plumas Ranch, you can hunt hogs over bait, which is typical in Texas. You can spot and stalk them, or hunt over water.

"In the summer, we offer discounted rates for hunting hogs because it is extremely hot down here," Williams said. "Summer is a great time for hunting hogs, especially for hunters who don't want to sit over bait or stalk them. They can sit over waterholes, like hunters do in the West when hunting elk over waterholes. Hogs need to drink lots of water in the summer and will regularly visit waterholes. Having a makeshift blind near a waterhole is a great option in the summer."

If you are adventuresome, you can hunt hogs with a knife. One hunter did that in our camp and came home with a giant 300-pound hog.

In Texas, hogs are a problem. If you don't like the idea of hunting on a ranch, consider knocking on farmers' doors. Many of them will be happy to let you chase hogs for a few bucks a day.

One of the nicest things about hunting hogs is the absence of pressure. You aren't chasing monster bucks and bulls. You are just chasing hogs so you can enjoy yourself and have fun bringing home the bacon.

The winter is the best time of year to go to Texas to hog hunt. If you are from the Midwest or East, there aren't many animals to hunt in the winter. By going south, you escape the cold and keep your archery skills sharp as a tack. I think I just persuaded myself to go hog hunting again!

• • • Go Exotic • • •

If you have ever dreamed of shooting an exotic critter like a goat or fallow deer, Texas is a great place to do that. Many of the ranches don't offer whitetail hunting, but they do offer hunting for exotics. You can purchase a package for hogs and exotics.

If you don't feel like going to Texas to chase hogs, you can find them almost anywhere. Many places throughout the Midwest offer Russian boar and feral hog hunting. The prices are reasonable, the hunting is fun, and the meat is great.

BIG GAME ON A BUDGET

The author with a nice bird he shot in the mountains of Colorado.

9

THE TRAVELING TURKEY HUNTER

When I speak at wild game dinners, fundraisers, and other events, people frequently ask about my favorite animal to hunt. I think most folks assume my answer will be big whitetail bucks. Although I do enjoy chasing whitetails, my favorite animal to go after is the wild turkey. I am sure some of you reading this might have just gasped for air or figured there is a typo in this book. It's not a typo. If I had to give up hunting everything but one critter, the critter I would keep chasing would be the wild turkey.

There is something about a strutting tom gobbling from the roost in spring that causes my heart to skip a beat. I have hunted turkey most of my life, and one thing that has remained constant from the time I started chasing them is I always shake like a leaf when I am about to get a shot. The adrenalin rush I get keeps me coming back for more.

The author's friend carries out a bird killed in the mountains of New Mexico.

A couple more reasons I enjoy hunting turkeys is they are fun to call in and the success rate in most states is extremely high. Some states even allow hunters to harvest two or more birds each spring, which makes hunting them even more fun.

Every year, I turkey hunt in about four or five states. One thing that makes hunting in that many states doable is that turkey hunting on a budget is extremely easy. Unlike hunting big game animals, turkey tags are often available over-the-counter and they are reasonably priced. Deer tags, elk tags, moose tags, and other big game tags can often set you back several hundred dollars each. Turkey tags, on the other hand, often cost around $100 dollars and, in many cases, even less. Because tags are so inexpensive, going on an out-of-state turkey hunt with your children is a great option. They will get to enjoy the adventure, spend time with their parent, and you can do it for a few hundred dollars.

Another plus of turkey hunting is it doesn't usually take long to find and kill birds even when hunting in a new state. Have I ever hunted out of my home state and come home empty handed? Of course. A few years ago, I flew from Michigan all the way to Washington State to hunt and ended up not tagging a bird. It does happen. Overall, though, my out-of-state success rate on turkeys is extremely high, and that is because turkey numbers are high in most states.

People often ask me where they should go turkey hunting if they decide to go on an out-of-state hunt. The first place I tell them, without hesitation, is out West. If you live in the West then it is a different answer, but for those who live in the East or the Midwest, my answer is always "head west."

The author and his friend, John Schindlbeck, after a successful hunt in Florida. Hunting Osceolas in Florida is one of the most expensive turkey hunts there are because Osceolas are only found in Florida.

Many hunters dream of chasing bugling bulls in places like Colorado, New Mexico, or Idaho. All three of these states offer turkey hunting, and the truth is a turkey hunt in any one of these places would be extremely exciting for anyone who tries it.

One of the main reasons I enjoy turkey hunting out West is because the species of turkey that inhabits the western United States is the Merriam's. This species, in my opinion, is the most beautiful of all the turkey sub-species. They have bleached white tail fans that will cause your jaw to drop when you see one strutting across an open meadow or through the dark timber.

Bowhunting turkeys can be a lot of fun. In the spring and fall, tagging long beards with stick and string is very challenging.

The other reason I love turkey hunting out West is the land I get to hunt. One reason most people from the eastern U.S. want to elk hunt is they want to spend some time in the big mountains. When turkey hunting out West, that's exactly where you spend a lot of your time.

A few years ago, I hunted turkey in Colorado. It was late April—a perfect time to be in the mountains. The weather was warm, the backcountry was beautiful, and the turkeys were plentiful. Toward the end of my hunt, I shot a longbeard in a high mountain meadow. I was at about 9,000 feet. I will never forget watching that tom gobble with his buddies as they came strutting across the meadow. In the background, I could see amazing mountain scenery, elk, and mule deer.

If a Western turkey hunt sounds like fun to you, I suggest hunting on public land in the backcountry the same way many people hunt for elk. Pack in a few miles, stay in a tent, eat freeze-dried food. That way you will experience all the West has to offer. If that doesn't sound like fun, staying in a hotel or a travel trailer is also an option. Keep in mind that if you choose to stay in a hotel or a travel trailer and you want to hunt in the backcountry each day, you will have to start your day hours before sunrise so you can get back into the woods before daybreak. Hunting out West is nothing like the Midwest. Plan on a lot of walking if you hunt in the backcountry.

Another Western option is to find birds on the edges of cities and towns. These suburbia birds are often easier to pattern and hunt than backcountry birds.

Regardless if you choose to hunt in the suburbs or the backcountry, one thing I have learned about hunting turkeys out West is that most people who live there don't really get into turkey hunting. As a result, knocking on doors and getting permission to hunt from a rancher is not out of the question. Many ranchers will likely say no, but some will say yes.

If you are a bowhunter who likes to chase turkeys, then definitely go west. Many say that Merriam's aren't as intelligent as Eastern birds. Some may argue otherwise, but from what I have seen, Merriam's aren't as smart as Eastern turkeys. As a result, calling one within bow range can be easy. Getting to full draw even when you are not hunting from a blind seems to be easier when hunting Merriam's versus the other sub-species of wild turkeys.

Should you not want to travel a great distance to turkey hunt but want to experience hunting in other parts of the country, there are two states I would suggest: Nebraska and Kansas.

I have hunted Kansas in the spring and the fall, and I am always amazed at how many turkeys these two states have. Not only do they have many turkeys, they also have long seasons, giving you plenty of time to find and hunt birds.

In Kansas, you will find mostly the Eastern sub-species. In Nebraska, you will find Merriam's. Both states have plenty of public land, and getting permission from landowners isn't very difficult, either.

If you want to go after the Rio Grande species, the best place to hunt is Texas. Texas is loaded with turkeys. The downside of hunting in Texas is that most of the land is private and many ranchers will charge you to hunt their land. That said, I do know several friends who have knocked on doors and received permission to hunt Rios for little or no money. If you are willing to put in your time, gaining access to good land can be had.

Another option when hunting in Texas is to hunt with an outfitter. Turkey hunting with an outfitter isn't nearly as expensive as whitetail hunting, and when you go with an outfitter, your chances of tagging several birds is extremely high. Most guided turkey hunts are three days long.

The author and some friends with a beautiful bird taken in the Western mountains at Vermejo Park Ranch.

Unless you are on a quest to kill a turkey in every state, or for some reason want to kill a turkey in a certain state, there are a few things to consider when turkey hunting away from home.

The most important consideration is whether the state you want to hunt in has a lot of turkeys. Obviously, it is going to be easier to tag a bird in a state with lots of turkeys versus a state that doesn't have a large turkey population. To find out what states offer the best hunting, simply get online and start visiting game and fish websites. Call a biologist if you need to. Find out what the turkey populations are in the states you are considering and the success rate of turkey hunters in those states. The data may vary from year to year, but as a rule, some of the best turkey hunting states have been so for years.

BIG GAME ON A BUDGET

For instance, most people who chase the Eastern wild turkey know one of the best places to hunt them is in Missouri.

The good news is regardless of what state you choose, chances are you will find large amounts of turkeys and the probability of tagging out is extremely high, which makes turkey hunting a great first-time budget hunt for anyone who has never traveled far from home to hunt.

Tracy Breen

The mountains can bring a man to his knees. Make sure you are in shape before you go on a budget hunt.

10

PHYSICAL CONDITIONING 101

You have probably read how animal rights fanatics and anti-gun groups are trying to stop us from hunting. Many avid outdoorsmen worry about future restrictions on their ability to hunt. Although anti-hunters are a huge threat to hunting, the other threat that we don't often read about that keeps people out of the woods and ends hunting careers is obesity. Many of us who once were lean and mean suddenly find ourselves overweight. Of course, the more overweight we become, the more lethargic we are, which makes hunting more difficult. In fact, a study done a few years ago revealed that the average hunter does not travel more than a third of a mile from his truck when hunting. This is often because many hunters are overweight.

What keeps most hunters from exercising and losing weight is the fear of becoming a gym rat. However, according to Mark Paulsen, founder of Wilderness Athlete (a company that makes nutritional products for outdoorsmen) and the former strength and conditioning coach for the University of New Mexico, hunters don't need to be gym rats to lose weight and stay in good enough shape to chase turkeys in the backwoods and elk in the mountains.

"I tell people the only way they will be able to lose weight is to find an exercise they enjoy doing," says Paulsen. "After they discover that particular exercise, they need to do it 30 minutes a day, three times a week. It is all about getting the heart rate up and burning calories. There are many different ways to do that. I enjoy hiking; some may enjoy swimming or riding a bike."

Dragging a deer out of the woods or carrying a turkey over your shoulder for an extended period can leave average hunters gasping. If you are out of shape, this can be very dangerous. Every year in America, hunters have heart attacks in the woods. Those who want to reduce the chance of having health problems must stay active and eat right.

"The saying, 'If you don't use it, you lose' is a true statement," says Paulsen. "As we age, the only way to stay in good shape and reduce the chances of serious health problems is staying active. Many hunters like hunting because they enjoy being in the woods. Hunters should exercise in the woods. One routine that can help someone lose weight is hiking for a half-mile or mile. Stop occasionally to do five pushups. Eventually, five will turn into ten and ten will turn into twenty. Walking, rollerblading, and mountain biking are a few other options for those who want to get into shape for hunting season. Exercising can be fun. Finding an exercise that is fun to do is the key to success."

And losing weight is much easier when we eat right.

BIG GAME ON A BUDGET

"One reason people don't stick to eating right is because they set themselves up to fail. I never tell anyone to give up sweets altogether or to stop buying potato chips. Have those treats occasionally—in moderation. The rest of the time, eat lots of unprocessed food. I think people are afraid of green vegetables today. A diet high in fruit, vegetables, and venison is a great recipe for losing weight. The biggest thing to avoid is sugar. Processed foods are extremely high in sugar. Sugar contributes to many health problems, including cancer, diabetes, and even arthritis. One of the fastest ways to cut out sugar is to stop buying soft drinks and sport drinks. Cutting back on sugar and all processed foods can help a person shed weight and feel better, which will make hunting more enjoyable."

Another bad habit hunters get into is eating a big meal after the hunt.

"I stop eating for the day after six p.m. If I am hunting hard all day and walk several miles a day, I don't worry about eating late, but as a rule, I stop eating early in the evening," Paulsen noted.

If losing weight is something you want to do, realize the best time to do it is before hunting season; not during hunting season. I always get into a workout routine several months before hunting season, so when it is time to hike I am ready for it. Paulsen agrees with this method.

We all make time for hunting and watching sports, and most of us waste plenty of time online. Paulsen says we should make time for our health because once our health goes downhill, putting the car into reverse is extremely difficult.

••• *100 Pounds and Counting* •••

If you seek, look no further than Duran Martinez. Martinez has an outdoor radio program that airs in Michigan called Wild Michigan. Martinez is an avid hunter who gradually (over twenty years) gained lots of weight. In fear that he might not be able to hunt or that he might die young, Martinez went on a quest to lose weight. Mark Paulsen put Martinez on a strict exercise program, and Martinez started using Wilderness Athlete products. Over the last year, Martinez has lost close to 100 pounds.

"I feel like a new man," says Martinez. *"Chasing turkeys and climbing in and out of treestands is easier than ever now that I have lost the weight."*

BIG GAME ON A BUDGET

Drawing tags is one of the only ways a person on a budget can kill trophy animals. Floyd Green from Arizona waited years before drawing the Arizona elk tag he needed to tag this monster.

11

DRAWING TAGS

Bowhunters grab magazines off the racks at local grocery stores each year and see photos that inspire dreams and drooling. They see pages of monster bucks and bulls and lucky hunters who brought them home. Most of the time, hunters close the magazines and hang their heads, thinking that only the wealthy can harvest a buck or bull that size. If you ever thought that, you're wrong.

Go ahead and dream of tagging a big buck or monster bull elk—you can do it! It will take a little work, a little time, and a lot of patience, but in the end you might find yourself standing over the trophy of a lifetime. How can you harvest a big game animal without spending lots of money? You need to play the drawing game.

I hear people say that someday they will win the lotto and become rich. When asked if they play the lotto, they usually say no. How can they win if they don't play the game? If you want to find yourself nose to nose with a trophy class animal, you must play the game. The states that hold large numbers of trophy-class animals possess some type of drawing process that hunters must go through if they want to hunt big game. Many states offer over-the-counter tags for hunting areas that hold bucks and bulls that aren't trophy-class. To hold a tag in your hand for an area that contains record-class animals, you need to apply for tags annually.

Most states use a drawing process because the number of hunters interested in hunting a certain unit outweighs the number of quality animals in that area. By restricting the number of hunters in the area, an elk herd or deer herd can be managed for age and trophy class, resulting in hunters who draw tags and get an opportunity to score on quality animals. States that require a drawing boast more trophy-class animals than states that don't. Look at Arizona, New Mexico, and Utah. All three incorporate some type of drawing process and all three produce monster elk. Before hunters apply for tags, they need to be aware of the system that's in place for the state they want to hunt. There are three types: the bonus point system, the preference point system, and the random drawing system.

BONUS POINT SYSTEM

With the bonus point system, when hunters apply for a specific tag and don't draw that tag, they are given a bonus point for the next year, which means that next year their name gets thrown into the hat twice. Hunters will have a better chance of drawing a tag the second time around. Their chances of drawing a tag increase if they've applied for a few years. If they apply ten years in a row

BIG GAME ON A BUDGET

without drawing a tag for a certain hunt, they will have ten chances of having their name drawn.

PREFERENCE POINT SYSTEM

The preference point system has become one of the most popular methods of distributing tags, especially out West, where the number of hunters outnumbers the number of tags. Under the preference point system, it may take five points to draw a certain tag. With hunters earning only one point with each application year, it will take five years to draw a tag. Hunters will not be able to hunt until they earn five points. Colorado has become one of the most popular states to hunt elk and mule deer in the country, and that state has a preference point system in place. In certain units within Colorado, it may take ten or fifteen years to acquire an elk tag, however, hunters are guaranteed a tag once they acquire enough points. Colorado offers a great opportunity; if hunters want to hunt in a particular unit for elk that requires five preference points, they can apply for a point each year and hunt in an over-the-counter unit in Colorado while they are waiting. This guarantees them a place to hunt. Many states require hunters to pay for their preference points. Keep in mind that by the time you draw a tag in a state with a preference point system, you may have hundreds or even thousands of dollars invested in your tag.

RANDOM DRAWING

Some states don't have a point system. In New Mexico, hunters take a fair number of record-class bull elk each year. Therefore, many non-residents apply for a New Mexico archery elk tag year after year. New Mexico is set up to allow 22 percent of tags for elk, deer, and antelope to be sold to non-residents each year. When those numbers are fulfilled, they don't distribute any more tags to non-residents. Hunters could apply for years and not draw a tag, or they could draw a tag rather quickly. According to the hunters I know who have hunted in New Mexico, non-residents can expect to draw a tag about every other year. However, with the random drawing there aren't any guarantees. Their name only goes into the hat once, regardless of how long they have been applying.

Matt Guedes from Colorado with a nice mountain goat. Guedes had very little money into this animal because he drew the tag. In many places, a mountain goat hunt will cost close to ten thousand dollars or more if you go on a guided hunt.

ANOTHER OPTION

If hunters don't draw a tag in a state like New Mexico, they have another option: purchasing a landowner tag. Ranchers and farmers receive landowner tags that they can use or sell to non-residents. Most choose to sell them to non-residents. The price of the tag usually depends on the demand and the class of bucks or bulls expected in that unit. In New Mexico, hunters can expect to pay up to a few thousand dollars for a bull elk landowner tag. In Utah, where 400-class bulls are not uncommon, the tags can be purchased for up to $25,000. In New Mexico, outfitters enjoy obtaining preference over non-residents. If hunters hire a guide before applying for a tag, they can list their outfitter number on the application, which will give them a better chance of drawing a tag than they would have if they sent the application in on their own. Twenty-two percent of New Mexico tags go to non-residents. Twelve percent goes to outfitters.

BIG GAME ON A BUDGET

If a big whitetail is on your list of must-haves, Kansas is the place for you so long as you're willing to pay the price. Hunters can purchase landowner tags in Kansas for around $1,000.

LEARNING HOW TO PLAY

The drawing process can be a confusing one. Knowing when to apply, the number of preference points required to draw, and which units to apply for requires lots of time. If you enjoy doing research and figuring out where to hunt on your own, it is a relatively inexpensive game to play. Each state has a website that will provide the information hunters need to know, including deadlines, fees, and success rates categorized by unit. If you lack extra time to spend on the Internet doing research, you may consider hiring an application service such as Carter's Application Service.

Garth Carter, owner of the service, offers a magazine called *Huntin' Fool* that is a great tool for anyone interested in applying for tags out West or in Kansas. Carter publishes the magazine twelve times a year. Each issue features two states and tells readers when they need to apply, which units are best, and other trends that may be going on in that state that could affect hunters. The magazine costs $100 a year, which, according to most people who subscribe to it, is worth every penny.

Jerrod Lile from Trophy Taker, who has been playing the drawing game for a long time, believes *Huntin' Fool* is a terrific tool.

"I read each issue from cover to cover," says Lile. "Although I don't use the application service, the magazine provides me with all of the information I need to make educated decisions about which states and what units to apply for."

Members of *Huntin' Fool* can call the Carters any time to discuss different options on which states to apply. If hunters are too busy to do any of the research themselves, the Carters will apply for them. Hunters are charged an application fee for each species and state they apply to. The hunters need to tell the Carters where they want to hunt, and they will do all of the work. The beauty of the service is that the Carter family has hunted extensively all of the Western states. They can answer almost any question hunters can throw at them about hunting in the West. That, in itself, is worth the money to most hunters. Hunters like Lile enjoy the fact that once they draw a tag, they can call the Carter family and acquire a list of hunters who are subscribers of *Huntin' Fool* who drew the same tag.

"Many of the tags people are applying for are once-in-a-lifetime tags," says Lile. "When hunters receive the list of other hunters who have hunted particular units, most of them are very helpful and willing to tell new hunters where to go. Guys have given me actual GPS coordinates of places that held big bulls when they were there. That kind of information is priceless."

BACK-UP PLAN

Hunters state the biggest problem with the drawing process is waiting years and years to draw the tag they are applying for. Garth Carter says hunters can solve that problem by having a back-up plan.

"Some hunters fail to apply for tags because they don't want to wait ten years to draw a tag for their favorite unit," says Carter. "The solution is to apply for areas that are easier to draw for and areas that take a number of years to draw. Some of the best mule deer hunting in the country can be found in a few units in Colorado that bowhunters can draw on their first or second try,"

If you want to hunt elk in New Mexico, planning a back-up mule deer hunt in Colorado provides a great technique to apply for a draw hunt and hunt when you don't draw the tag you were anticipating.

"When hunters do research and see that an area is a draw unit, it doesn't necessarily mean they won't get a tag," Carter explains. "Draw units deter some hunters from applying; therefore, there are leftovers. For instance, almost every year Idaho has leftover Shiras Moose tags. Not everyone knows that. There are plenty of back-up options for hunters who apply for tags. When you become a member of our service, we will share that info with you."

Huntin' Fool can be used in another effective manner. Tom Johnson purchases *Huntin' Fool*, investigates their highlighted units, and determines the best units for him to hunt. He then tries to hunt as close to those units as possible in an area that offers over-the-counter tags.

"In Colorado, I especially like to use *Huntin' Fool* as a tool to find areas that are overlooked or don't carry bulls as big as the bulls in the draw units," says Johnson, "yet still hold nice animals. A draw unit might have 350-inch bulls, but there might be a unit close by that has 300-inch bulls and doesn't require you to draw a tag."

WHITETAIL BACK-UP PLANS

For those of you who can't get enough monster whitetails mounted on the wall, head to Kansas or Iowa. Both states have a lottery system, and it takes about two years to draw a tag in either state. After hunters draw a tag, getting a 150-class buck is possible. While you are waiting to draw a tag, you may want to consider states like Ohio or Wisconsin. In the last few years, numerous monster bucks have been harvested in Ohio. In Ohio, you can purchase tags over the counter. Wisconsin also holds large bucks and has over-the-counter tags available. The drawback to Wisconsin is many counties have an "Earn a Buck" program, which means that hunters must harvest a doe before they can kill a buck. Illinois also has great bucks, and while non-residents need to apply, they usually have leftover tags. Having a back-up plan allows you to hunt every year while you are waiting to draw that coveted tag in Kansas or Iowa.

COST

If you are a blue-collar American, one of the biggest problems with the drawing process is the amount of money that needs to be spent applying for tags. A $25 application fee is required in various states. Others charge the entire tag fee and reimburse you months later when you learn that you were unsuccessful at drawing. Lile has found a solution to the money crunch.

"Every year," he explains, "just before I start applying for tags, I take one of those credit card applications that offers zero percent interest for six months or a year and apply for all of my tags. All of my money will come back before the zero percent offer is up, and then I pay off the card," Lile explained.

The process doesn't hurt as much when you use a credit card like Lile does, but no matter what you do, if you apply for multiple states and species, you will incur costs. Every state has an application fee.

PATIENCE

Having patience and waiting a few years to draw the tag of your dreams can be tough for hunters who want everything now, but your patience will be rewarded if you wait long enough. According to Carter, you could end up with the tag and a critter that typically only the rich can afford.

"Many hunters believe killing an animal with a large rack is a game for the rich," says Carter. "When you play the drawing game, you can end up with a great tag and a great animal that might be as big if not bigger than an animal that a wealthy hunter paid thousands for. The regular guy can still kill big animals; he just needs to know the system."

For many hunters like Lile and Johnson, the drawing process becomes part of the hunt. During the winter and spring—when most states require you to send in your application—there isn't a bow season open. Researching and learning where to go to find big-antlered animals is fun and gives you something to do during the off-season.

Most hunters who have been applying in multiple states for years draw a tag almost every year or every other year. If hunters apply for special tags this year, it may take a few years to draw tags; however, once they do they will be off to a new, exciting place regularly with a chance of bagging a trophy-class animal. Regardless, if you are after a trophy bull elk, a nice mule deer, or a dandy whitetail, start applying for non-resident tags and your hunting wishes just might come true!

EPILOGUE

I did not intend, in writing this book, to provide you with all the information you need to know to start hunting across North America. Instead, I wrote it to give you a brief overview on how to hunt some of today's most popular big game animals on a budget. The book should be informative and inspire you, the reader, so you know that you can make your hunting dreams come true. Every hunter I interviewed for this book is someone who chooses to hunt on a budget. As you read each chapter and looked at the pictures, my hope is it lit a spark in you to plan a hunt in an unfamiliar place. Hunting in our own backyard is fun, but hunting on a mountainside or in a river bottom you have never entered before can be exhilarating.

Happy hunting...and God bless!

Tracy Breen

APPENDIX

One thing that can quickly turn a budget hunt into an expensive hunt is gear. Most quality hunting gear costs a small fortune. Unfortunately, buying inexpensive gear isn't really an option when hunting off the beaten path. When I started traveling to hunting destinations all over the country, I bit the bullet and purchased the best gear money could buy, knowing that the gear would pay me back and then some if I kept it for years and was able to use it repeatedly. Because I am always trying to stay on budget, and since I know most of you reading this are likely trying to do the same, I will only discuss what gear you must have and leave out the gear that would be helpful to have. If I included all the gear I would like to have, this book would be twice as long and my bank account would be empty.

SHELTER

First, you need a quality shelter. Whether you are elk hunting in the mountains or deer hunting in the Midwest, if you are trying to do it without spending much money, you will want to tent camp. A hotel or lodge can break the bank.

My favorite type of backcountry shelter is a tipi. There are several brands on the market today; the one I use is made by a company in Colorado called Kifaru. There are a few reasons I choose to use a tipi versus a conventional tent. Number one, a tipi is much simpler. It can be set up even in a strong wind without much problem because there is only one pole, which is a center pole. Besides the pole, you only have stakes that are required to set it up. Second, a tipi can accommodate a wood stove. My tipi came with a collapsible wood stove that is extremely lightweight, doesn't take up much space, and can heat up my tipi in no time. I dry out my clothes over the stove, cook food on the stove, and use the stove to keep myself warm, which is extremely important when the weather gets bad. Best of all, a four-man tipi and the stove do not weigh much more than five pounds. The only drawback of a tipi is it doesn't have a floor.

The author often uses a Kifaru Tipi when hunting in the backcountry.

When I am hunting in an area with lots of biting insects, I use a regular lightweight tent because I don't want to be kept up at night with mosquitos buzzing in my ear or spiders crawling up my pant leg.

A good sleeping bag and mat goes hand-in-hand with a good shelter. I use a Cabela's sleeping mat and have a Eureka lightweight sleeping bag. Notice I said lightweight. I only use a sleeping bag and mat when hunting in the backcountry. Therefore, I need something that is lightweight, compact, and comfortable. All these traits can cost a lot of money, but at the end of the day, a good night's rest is worth it. If you take care of your shelter, sleeping bag, and mat, they

BIG GAME ON A BUDGET

can last you decades, so consider purchasing high-end products an investment.

FOOTWEAR

Next on my list of must-haves is a pair of high-quality boots. I mentioned how necessary good boots are earlier in the book. Without good boots, your hunt is over. It is that simple. Nothing can ruin a hunt like blood blisters. Over the years, I have learned this the hard way.

Another reason you will want good boots is because cheap boots leak. When feet get wet, they start to rub against the side of your socks and the side of the boot, which can cause blisters. Also, wet feet often become cold feet and when feet get cold, it is hard to concentrate on hunting.

Having cerebral palsy makes my feet extremely sensitive. It doesn't take much for my feet and ankles to start to ache. Good boots reduce the amount of pain I am in, especially when walking long distances in the mountains. Walking sidehill can be hard on anyone's feet, and the better your boots the more miles you will be able to walk without running into trouble.

Never skimp when purchasing boots. A good pair of boots can make or break the hunt. A pair of Schnee's boots like these can cost a lot of money but they will last for years. (photo courtesy Schnee's; schnees.com)

I use Schnee's boots. Made in Montana, they are built to last. I can ruin a pair of boots in a little over a year, but I have had the same pair of Schnee's Boots for four years and they are still going strong. I have elk hunted in them several times, chased mountain lions, mule deer, and many other animals. I think they have several years left in them before I will need another pair.

BACKPACK

Another item all backcountry hunters need is a high-quality backpack. I always tell people that a good pack will make an 80-pound load feel like 40 pounds and a bad pack will make a 40-pound load feel like 80 pounds. A good backpack, one that you can use for years, will cost hundreds of dollars, but a good backpack isn't just another piece of gear. It is a long-term investment. A backpack is a tool that helps you get your most precious cargo—meat—out of the woods. When looking at backpacks, make sure you get a pack that has a meat shelf for easily packing meat out of the woods. Make sure it has plenty of pockets and a place to hold a water bladder. Make sure the largest compartment is big enough to hold a week's worth of food and gear if you intend to use it on a long hunt. I like a pack that has over 5500 cubic inches of storage. If I plan on going on a long trip, I like a pack that has over 6500 cubic inches of storage. My pack is made by Outdoorsmans in Phoenix, Arizona. The Outdoorsman Pack is durable, American-made, and isn't extremely heavy. When purchasing a pack, it is important to note that the weight of the pack when empty is something you will want to pay attention to. I have seen some great packs that I wouldn't use because they feel like a boat anchor when they are strapped to my back. Finding a pack that isn't super heavy and is built to last is extremely important.

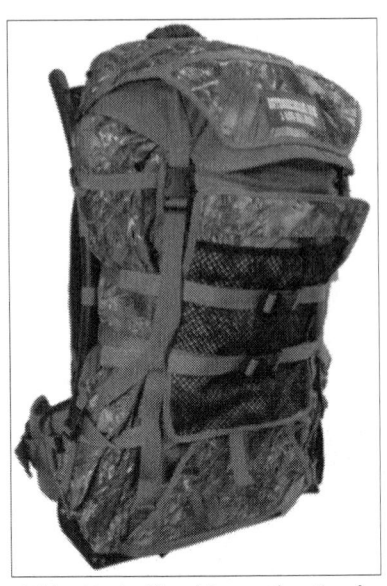

A lightweight, durable pack is a must-have piece of gear. The pack shown here is an Outdoorsmans Pack. (photo courtesy Outdoorsmans; outdoorsmans.com

BIG GAME ON A BUDGET

FOOD

The food you bring on a trip is also important. When I am hunting whitetails or turkeys, I bring a cooler filled with lunchmeat and bread with a few protein bars for variety. When I am hunting in the backcountry, I bring only food that is lightweight and packed with protein. My favorite type of food to bring into the deep woods is Mountain House freeze-dried food. Mountain House is the most trusted brand of freeze-dried food on the market. When you add boiling water to the food, it is ready to eat in a few minutes. Best of all, the stuff tastes great and is packed with protein. Mountain House offers a wide selection of meals, including breakfast and dessert. It is important to note that having a few snacks and dessert can really boost your spirits after a week of eating the same thing every day. A sweet treat occasionally can keep you in the right mindset. Being far from home, eating plain food, and hiking for miles every day without tagging an animal can wear on the mind and the body. Little things like pudding or a candy bar can help you keep on keeping on.

A tipi can be purchased with a collapsable wood stove.

Along with freeze-dried food and snacks, I always bring Wilderness Athlete Energy & Focus and Hydrate & Recover. These two powdered drink mixes keep me energized and hydrated. Dehydration can quickly get dangerous, especially when hunting miles from a good water source. Adding Wilderness Athlete to your water gives it good flavor and keeps you hydrated, which is extremely important when hiking miles every day. Staying hydrated can also reduce your chances of getting altitude sickness.

While I am on the subject of altitude sickness, Wilderness Athlete makes an herbal supplement called Altitude Advantage that I always take when hiking and hunting in the mountains. The supplement has not failed me yet. I used to get altitude sickness every time I hunted in the high country. Now I rarely have any symptoms.

CLOTHING

If you are a whitetail hunter going on a whitetail or turkey hunt, chances are you already know how to dress. If you are going on a Western hunt for the first time, you may not know what clothes to bring and what to wear. Buying the proper clothing for a Western hunt is where things can get expensive. That said, if you are frugal, you don't have to break the bank if you purchase only what you need.

The problem with hunting out West or in the far North is you can have extreme temperature variations. You can wake up one day and it is 20 degrees outside with a high of 40 degrees, then wake up the next day and the temperature is a high of 70 degrees. With temperature swings like this, it is easy to be overdressed or underdressed. If you are overdressed and have to take a few layers off, it isn't a big deal. If you are underdressed, getting hypothermia is a possibility. The solution to both problems is to wear layers. My favorite way to dress is by wearing mostly wool clothing.

Many companies make great wool clothes that work well in cold and warm weather. I will wear a thin base layer and a thicker outer layer. Wool retains heat even when wet, so regardless if I sweat a little or it rains a little, wool will help keep me warm.

Another reason I like wearing wool is that it is quiet when stalking big game and it doesn't give off ultraviolet light like a lot of hunting clothes. Best of all, modern day merino wool is comfortable to wear, dries out when wet much faster than the wool used for World War II army clothes, and it is extremely long-lasting.

If you are on a budget, a couple tops and a couple pairs of pants is almost all that is needed for a ten-day hunt. I will hunt in one set

BIG GAME ON A BUDGET

of clothes for a couple days and then let them hang outside for a couple days while I wear another set. This routine has worked well for me.

ELECTRONIC DEVICES

There are a few electronic devices I never leave home without. Number one is a quality GPS unit. There is a wide variety of GPS units on the market. I use the Garmin 650T. This high-end GPS has every bell and whistle you can think of. My favorite feature is the fact that you can download maps onto the GPS. OnXmaps out of Montana offers plat maps that show public and private land and the names of the landowners like a traditional printed plat book. These maps come in handy when hunting out West in areas where you are unsure where the property lines are. Ranchers often post public land as private, so having the OnXmaps can help you focus on where the property lines are, which may help you fill a tag.

Regardless of what kind of GPS you purchase, get familiar

A top-notch GPS, such as this Garmin 650T, is a must when hunting on your own. (photo courtesy Garmin; garmin.com)

with it long before you head out on a hunting trip. If you don't know how to use your GPS, it will do you no good. If you know how to use it, it is one of the most important tools to have in your pocket while hunting.

I don't leave home without a SPOT device, either. A SPOT is a satellite messenger that can save your life. It has a couple features I really like. It has a button that allows you to send an OK message to your friends and family. If you are in the backcountry without any cell service, you can hit the OK button and it sends an email with your GPS coordinates attached and an X on the map, so to speak, so everyone knows where you are.

The device also has a 911 button. If you get into trouble, you hit this button and the device sends a distress message to the local authorities. If you break your leg and can't walk, you have a way of letting everyone know you need help. The device and the yearly service is a little pricey, but it is well worth the peace of mind.

OTHER ITEMS

Other key items I don't leave home without include a couple tarps, duct tape, a compass, a high-quality knife, a bone saw, and a knife sharpening kit. If I am hunting in the backcountry, I also bring paracord for hanging game bags. You can buy inexpensive game bags and get by, but I prefer buying bags that keep the insects off the meat and don't easily rip. Alaska Game Bags, Caribou Game Bags, and Walhog Wilderness Bags are a few of my favorites. Walhog Wilderness makes a meat spray called MeatSavr that I bring with me as well when hunting in the backcountry. This spray keeps insects off the meat and protects the meat from spoiling.

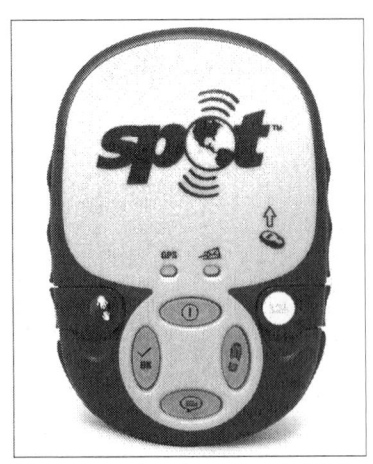

The author never leaves home without the SPOT device. This emergency device can save your life. (photo courtesy SPOT LLC; findmespot.com)

This appendix could go on and on because the amount of gear I like to bring with me on a trip is endless, yet I wanted to provide you with the must-haves, not the wants. If I were to bring everything I wanted on a hunting trip, I would need a string of pack mules and four or five ATVs. Being lean and mean when you leave the trail is necessary.

BIG GAME ON A BUDGET

Tracy Breen

Made in the USA
Charleston, SC
29 January 2015